# Make the Show

*How to Start a Podcast, Build a Real Audience, and Make a Show Worth Coming Back To*

**Mike Hamilton**

# Copyright

Make the Show: How to Start a Podcast, Build a Real Audience, and Make a Show Worth Coming Back To



Published by Rogue Media Network

Waco, Texas

thatmikehamilton.com

ISBN: 979-8-90599-626-9

First Edition, 2026

Disclaimer: This book is for informational and educational purposes only. Nothing in this book constitutes legal, financial, medical, or professional advice. The author is not a lawyer. For any situation involving legal, financial, or other professional risk, consult a qualified professional. Platform policies, tools, and technologies referenced in this book are subject to change; verify current information before making decisions based on specific platform guidance.

Printed in the United States of America

# About the Author

**Mike Hamilton** is the co-founder and Chief Creative Officer of Rogue Media Network, a podcast and media company based in Waco, Texas. Since 2019, he has helped build, launch, and produce more than 150 shows across sports, horror, true crime, local storytelling, business, entertainment, and independent media. Through ThatMikeHamilton.com, he helps Gen X and older audiences use AI and new technology without pretending they were born online.

Mike has spent most of his career building things at the intersection of media, storytelling, and practical tools — and watching a lot of people talk themselves out of making the show they wanted to make. This book is his attempt to make that harder to do.

He lives in Waco with more cables than he needs and at least one project he has not started yet.

Find him at thatmikehamilton.com and at Rogue Media Network wherever you listen to podcasts.

# Dedication

For everyone who kept carrying the idea.

Make the show.

*The work adds up long before the result becomes visible.*

— Mike Hamilton

# Contents

Chapter 25: Start Simple. Tell the Truth. Keep Going.

# Introduction

Let's get something out of the way before we start.

You do not have to make a show.

You really don't.

There are plenty of good reasons not to.

You're busy.

You're tired.

You have a job.

You have a family.

You have bills.

You have people who need things from you.

You have a garage that needs cleaning, a doctor's appointment you keep moving, a streaming show you started three months ago and still swear you're going to finish, and some random drawer in your house full of cables that may or may not belong to devices you still own.

You might not like the sound of your voice.

You might not know what microphone to buy.

You might not know how to edit.

You might not want to be on video.

You might think you're too late.

You might think podcasting is already too crowded.

You might think nobody cares what you have to say.

You might think the technology moved too fast and now everybody else knows something you don't.

You might look at YouTube, TikTok, Spotify, Apple Podcasts, AI tools, clips, captions, thumbnails, algorithms, websites, email lists, sponsorships, and all of that and think:

"Nope. I'm good."

And honestly?

Fair.

That is a perfectly reasonable reaction.

There is no shortage of reasons to not do this.

But if the idea keeps coming back, that matters.

If you keep thinking, "I should tell this story," that matters.

If you keep saying, "Somebody ought to make a show about this," maybe that somebody is you.

If you keep watching other people make things and thinking, "I could do that better," or "I have a different angle," or "They're missing the real story," then maybe it is time to stop sitting in the stands yelling at the field.

Maybe it is time to make the show.

Not a perfect show.

Not a giant show.

Not a show with a studio that looks like it was designed by a tech company with too much purple lighting.

A real show.

Your show.

That is what this book is about.

Not just starting a podcast.

Making a show.

There is a difference.

A podcast sounds like something you upload.

A show sounds like something you make.

A show has shape. A show has a promise. A show has a beginning, a middle, and an end. A show gives people a reason to come back. A show feels like someone cared enough to build it.

That is the mindset I want you to have.

We are not just tossing audio files into the wind and hoping the internet burps out an audience.

We are making shows.

They may be audio-only.

They may be video.

They may be both.

They may be interview shows, solo shows, co-hosted shows, local shows, business shows, storytelling shows, fiction shows, weird little late-night shows that only make sense to the right people.

Fine.

Good.

The world does not need more generic content.

It needs more specific, useful, honest, human shows made by people who actually care.

## A Word About Gen X

I should probably say this early.

I do not really love generational labels.

Gen X. Gen Z. Millennials. Boomers. Whatever else somebody in marketing is going to invent next so they can sell us insurance, sneakers, meal kits, or a truck during halftime.

I get why the labels exist. They are shortcuts. They help researchers, advertisers, and media people group things together.

But people are not that clean.

People are not little boxes.

We are not all red or blue, black or white, young or old, analog or digital, this or that.

Most people are shades of gray.

Most people are just trying to live their lives, take care of the people they love, get through the day, be decent when they can, and figure out the next right thing.

So when I talk about Gen X in this book, I am not trying to shove anybody into a cage.

I am using it as a doorway.

I am talking to people who remember one version of the world and are now trying to create in another.

People who remember when shows felt like shows.

ABC. NBC. CBS. Fox.

MTV when it still played music videos.

Saturday morning cartoons.

Appointment television.

Reruns.

Video stores.

Mixtapes.

Landlines.

Three channels if the antenna was behaving and somebody was standing in the right spot.

We grew up with shows.

Not "content."

Shows.

A show came on at a certain time. You either watched it or you missed it. There was no pause button. There was no "skip intro." There was no algorithm feeding you fifteen more things exactly like the last thing you watched until your brain turned into pudding.

You waited.

You showed up.

You talked about it the next day.

That does not mean the old days were better in every way. They weren't. Let's not get carried away and pretend adjusting rabbit ears was a spiritual experience.

But we did learn something from that world.

We learned that shows have identity.

They have openings.

They have endings.

They have rhythm.

They have tone.

They have a feel.

You knew when you were watching a sitcom, a drama, a news magazine, a late-night show, a sports show, a cartoon, a variety show, or some strange cable thing you found at midnight and never forgot.

That matters now.

Because the tools have changed, but people still want shows.

They still want something worth coming back to.

They still want a voice they recognize.

They still want a story.

They still want to learn something, laugh at something, argue with something, or feel less alone for twenty minutes.

That has not changed.

## Why This Book Exists

Podcasting used to feel simpler.

You got a microphone. You recorded. You uploaded. You hoped people listened.

Now everything feels bigger and stranger.

Should it be audio?

Should it be video?

Should it be on YouTube?

Should it be on Spotify?

Should it have clips?

Should it have transcripts?

Should it have a website?

Should AI help write the show notes?

Should AI edit the clips?

Should you sell sponsors?

Should you start a newsletter?

Should you use your face on the cover?

Should you record in your closet?

Should you buy the expensive mic?

Should you wait until you understand all of it?

No.

Please do not wait until you understand all of it.

That is how shows die before they start.

This book is meant to help you sort through the noise.

It is for first-time creators.

It is for people who tried before and quit.

It is for people who have been carrying a show idea around for years like an old cassette tape in a glove box.

It is for people who know they have something to say but are not sure where to begin.

It is for business owners, storytellers, teachers, coaches, local experts, retired people, second-act creators, parents, grandparents, movie people, sports people, true crime people, faith people, funny people, weird people, tired people, and people who have lived long enough to know that life gets complicated and stories come from complication.

It is especially for people who remember the old media world but are willing to use the new tools.

That is a powerful place to stand.

You do not have to pretend you were born online.

You do not have to dance for the algorithm.

You do not have to become some fake version of yourself because a social media expert with a ring light said that was the future.

You can use the tools.

You can use AI.

You can use video.

You can use podcast hosting, websites, clips, newsletters, search, sponsors, and whatever else helps.

But the tools should serve the show.

Not the other way around.

## What Is Inside This Book

This book is not here to impress you with jargon.

It is not here to bury you in charts.

It is not here to tell you that if you follow seven secret steps, you will have a million downloads, a national sponsor, a merch store, and people stopping you in airports.

That is nonsense.

This book is here to help you start clearly, build smart, and keep going.

We are going to talk about what you are actually making before you buy a microphone.

We are going to talk about why your show needs a promise.

We are going to talk about gear without turning it into a shopping addiction.

We are going to talk about audio, video, and short clips without pretending one format magically solves everything.

We are going to talk about naming the show without getting so cute nobody knows what it is.

We are going to talk about cover art that works when it is tiny, because most people are not seeing your masterpiece on a movie screen. They are seeing a little square on a phone while waiting for tacos.

We are going to talk about hosting, RSS feeds, websites, YouTube, Spotify, Apple, and why your show needs a home base.

We are going to talk about search and discoverability, not as tricks, but as clarity.

We are going to talk about structure: openings, endings, interviews, co-hosts, soundchecks, and why a show should feel like somebody is driving.

We are going to talk about your voice, and why the first time you hear yourself recorded you may briefly consider changing your name and moving to a town where nobody knows you.

We are going to talk about Resistance.

Overthinking.

Research rabbit holes.

Perfectionism.

Podfade.

The thing that makes people quit.

We are going to talk about audience growth without chasing everybody.

We are going to talk about sponsors, money, house ads, free trials, founding sponsors, and how to look sponsor-ready before the sponsor money shows up.

We are going to talk about AI and how to let it carry some of the weight without letting it steal your voice.

We are going to talk about sustainability, because starting is one thing, but building a show you can keep making when life gets annoying is the real work.

And there is a companion workbook — worksheets, checklists, emails, sponsor templates, guest outreach forms, AI prompts, and planning tools you can actually use — available separately at thatmikehamilton.com/workbook.

Because I do not want this to just be a book you read and then put on a shelf.

I want it to be something you mark up, steal from, argue with, use, spill coffee on, and maybe keep near the toilet.

Let's be honest.

This book goes great with toilet time.

Some of the best decisions in human history have probably been made in there. Some of the worst too, but we will focus on the positive.

## The Reasons Not to Do This

Before we go any further, let's honor the reasons not to make the show.

Because they are real.

You may not have time.

You may not have money.

You may not have confidence.

You may not have support.

You may not have technical skills.

You may not have an audience.

You may not have a perfect idea.

You may not know if the show should be audio, video, or both.

You may not like how you look on camera.

You may not like how you sound.

You may worry people will judge you.

They might.

You may worry nobody will listen.

At first, maybe not many will.

You may worry the show will be bad.

The first version might be.

You may worry someone else is already doing it.

Someone probably is.

You may worry you are too old to start.

You are not.

You may worry you are too late.

You are not.

You may worry the world does not need another show.

The world may not need another generic show.

But it may need yours.

That is the difference.

If your only goal is fame, this book may disappoint you.

If your only goal is to get rich fast, there are probably easier ways to become miserable.

If you want a magic formula, I do not have one.

If you want to avoid work, this is the wrong book.

But if you want to make something real, useful, entertaining, honest, sustainable, and yours, then we can work with that.

## Come to Terms With It

So here is what I want you to do.

Come to terms with the reasons not to do it.

Do not pretend they are not there.

Look at them.

Name them.

Write them down if you need to.

Time.

Money.

Fear.

Technology.

Voice.

Video.

Editing.

Embarrassment.

Age.

Confidence.

Whatever it is.

Get honest.

Then ask the better question:

Is this a reason to quit, or is this a problem to solve?

Because those are different.

If you do not have time, maybe the show needs to be shorter.

If you do not have money, maybe the starter setup needs to be simple.

If you hate video, maybe start audio-only.

If you hate editing, maybe build a cleaner format or get help.

If you do not know what to say, maybe you need a pre-production meeting with yourself.

If you are afraid nobody will care, maybe you need to find the first ten people instead of chasing everybody.

If you are scared the first version will be bad, good news: it might be.

Then you make the second one better.

That is how this works.

Not perfectly.

Honestly.

The goal is not to eliminate every reason to be afraid.

The goal is to stop letting fear run the meeting.

## Open the Damn Book

So if you are looking for one more excuse, I am sure you can find one.

We are all very creative when we want to avoid doing something that matters.

You can research microphones until your eyes cross.

You can compare hosting platforms like you are choosing a college for your child.

You can change the name twelve times.

You can ask people who would never listen to the show whether they like the idea.

You can wait for the perfect time.

You can wait until work slows down.

You can wait until the kids are older.

You can wait until you feel ready.

You can wait until the world becomes less weird.

Good luck with that last one.

Or you can open the damn book and read it.

Then do the next thing.

Not the whole thing.

The next thing.

Write the idea.

Name the audience.

Record the test.

Pick the format.

Make the first episode.

Listen back.

Fix what you can.

Publish when it is ready enough.

Make the next one better.

That is the system.

Start simple.

Tell the truth.

Keep going.

Now let's make the show.

# How to Use This Book

This book has 25 chapters, 39 worksheets, and 13 templates. That sounds like a lot. It is a lot. You do not have to do all of it at once, and you definitely do not have to do it in order.

Here is how to think about what is in here.

## The Three Parts

**Part One: Build the Show (Chapters 1–11)**

Start here. These chapters cover why your voice matters, how the media landscape got where it is, what you are actually making, what format to choose, gear, naming, cover art, where the show lives, and how people find it. If you have never made a show before, read these in order.

**Part Two: Run the Show (Chapters 12–19)**

Structure, hosting, voice, operations, sustainability, audience growth, and launch. These chapters are about making the show feel built and keeping it alive. Dip in as you need them.

**Part Three: Protect and Grow the Show (Chapters 20–25)**

Legal basics, money, AI, show expansion, and the long game. Read Chapter 20 before you take a sponsor. Read Chapter 21 before you chase revenue. Read Chapter 23 when AI starts feeling like a shortcut that worries you.

## The Companion Workbook

This book has a companion workbook — 39 worksheets, 13 templates, a Show Bible Starter, and ready-to-use emails for everything from guest outreach to sponsor pitches. It is available as a standalone PDF at:

**thatmikehamilton.com/workbook**

Download it, print it, fill it in, lose it, print it again. Each worksheet is numbered to match the chapter that references it. If you only use five, start with these:

- **Worksheet 1** — Why This Show Needs to Exist *(start here)*
- **Worksheet 2** — The Show Promise *(do this before anything else)*
- **Worksheet 4** — Enough-to-Start Gear Plan *(before you spend money)*
- **Worksheet 14** — Podfade Prevention Plan *(before the show gets heavy)*
- **Worksheet 21** — Final Launch Card *(before you publish)*

## Quick Path by Goal

Not sure where to start? Find your situation below.

*Worksheet numbers below refer to the companion workbook at thatmikehamilton.com/workbook.*

**"I just want to start a show."**

Read Chapters 1–3. Fill out Worksheets 1–3. Record a five-minute test. Then come back.

**"I have an idea but do not know the format."**

Read Chapters 3–7. Fill out Worksheets 2 and 5. Make a decision. Revisit after ten episodes.

**"I am almost ready to launch."**

Read Chapters 17–18. Fill out Worksheets 15, 20, and 21. Go.

**"I want sponsors."**

Read Chapters 20–21. Fill out Worksheets 16–18 and 29–30. Do not pitch before the show is sponsor-ready.

**"I keep almost quitting."**

Read Chapters 16 and 24. Fill out Worksheets 13 and 14. Do this now, not later.

**"I want to use AI without losing my voice."**

Read Chapter 23. Fill out Worksheet 19. Build a prompt library.

## One More Thing

This book was written to be used, not just read.

Mark it up. Dog-ear the pages. Write in the margins. Argue with the advice. Get the workbook at thatmikehamilton.com/workbook and fill that in too.

A book you read once and shelved taught you something.

A book you keep coming back to builds a show.

## Get the Workbook

The companion workbook is available as a standalone PDF at **thatmikehamilton.com/workbook**. It is a separate product from this book — download it, print it, write in it, use it however it works for you.

# Chapter 1: Your Voice Still Matters

If you made it through the introduction and you are still here, congratulations.

That means one of two things.

Either you actually want to make a show, or you are avoiding something else and this book is now part of your procrastination system.

Either way, welcome.

Let's start with the thing I believe most:

Your voice still matters.

Not because the world is sitting around breathlessly waiting for every thought you have. It is not. The world is busy. The world is loud. The world has laundry to fold, bills to pay, kids to pick up, emails to ignore, and at least one streaming service asking if we are still watching like it is judging our life choices.

Your voice matters because there is probably someone out there who needs the specific thing you can bring.

Not everyone.

Probably not everyone.

That is fine.

Everyone is too big anyway.

Everyone is a stadium full of strangers who all want different snacks.

You are not trying to reach everyone.

You are trying to reach the right someone.

Somebody needs the story you keep almost telling.

Somebody needs the lesson you learned the hard way.

Somebody needs the interview you are afraid to ask for.

Somebody needs your explanation because you explain things in a way that makes sense to them.

Somebody needs your humor.

Somebody needs your warning.

Somebody needs your encouragement.

Somebody needs your memory of how things used to be and your willingness to figure out how things work now.

That is the part that matters.

Not the microphone.

Not the software.

Not the cover art.

Not whether you understand every new platform that showed up while you were trying to find the right HDMI cable.

The human part matters first.

The tools come later.

## You Have Lived Through Something

One of the reasons I wanted this book to lean toward the Gen X crowd, even though I do not love the label, is because people in this general stage of life have lived through a strange amount of change.

We remember the old media world.

We remember when a show came on and you either watched it or you missed it. We remember when MTV actually played music videos, which feels like saying, "I remember when Pizza Hut had red cups," but both things matter in their own way. We remember appointment television, video stores, mixtapes, landlines, cable boxes, newspapers, magazines, and trying to record something on a VCR without accidentally taping over something important.

We also watched the internet show up.

We watched computers move from school-lab weirdness to something everyone had to learn. We watched email become normal. We watched websites become necessary. We watched phones become cameras, maps, calendars, televisions, radios, wallets, newspapers, game systems, and little rectangles of anxiety that live in our pockets.

Now we are watching AI walk into the room and act like it has always been invited to Thanksgiving.

That is a lot.

And the easy mistake is to think all of that change means we are behind.

I do not buy that.

Experience changes what knowledge means.

That may not sound as sharp as a rock-star quotation, but it is true.

There is a version of knowledge that lives entirely in books, courses, podcasts, and other people's case studies. It is clean and organized and has never been field-tested. It sounds good until life puts actual weight on it.

Then there is knowledge that comes from mileage. From actually doing the thing. From failing at versions one through four before five worked. From sitting in the parking lot before the hard conversation. From the show that got canceled. The job that fell apart. The thing you thought you understood until you had to live through it.

That second kind is what you have.

The mileage shows up in the stories.

It shows up in knowing what actually matters versus what just sounds like it does.

It shows up in the way you explain something to a person who is panicking, because you have panicked about the same thing and you remember what helped.

I think it means we have context.

We remember before and after.

That gives us perspective.

We know what it was like when media felt scarce. We know what it feels like now when media is everywhere and somehow still hard to trust. We know what it means to wait for a show, to talk about a show, to follow a story, to recognize a voice, to care about a host, to feel like a program has a real identity.

That is useful now.

Because the platforms have changed, but people have not changed as much as everyone pretends.

People still want stories.

People still want to laugh.

People still want to understand something.

People still want to feel less alone.

People still want someone to say the thing plainly.

People still want a place to come back to.

That is a show.

That is not old-fashioned.

That is human.

## I Started With the Same Thing

I started Rogue Media Network in 2019 because I loved podcasting.

That is the short version.

The longer version is that I loved what it could become.

I loved the idea that a person could sit down with a microphone, a story, a point of view, a weird obsession, a mission, a memory, or a reason to say something out loud, and turn that into a real thing.

A show.

Not a giant television production.

Not something that had to go through a boardroom full of people who all use words like “synergy” with a straight face.

Just a show.

A real show.

Something that started as nothing and then, with enough work, existed.

That has always been one of my favorite feelings in the world. I love making things out of nothing. I love drawing. I love movies. I love television. I love old cartoons. I love audio fiction. I love the moment when an idea stops being just a thing in your head and starts becoming something someone else can hear, watch, read, share, argue with, laugh at, or carry around for a while.

That was a big reason I wanted to start Rogue.

I wanted to make audio fiction.

That was the dream.

But dreams have bills attached.

So we built a network. We recorded shows. We edited. We rented spaces. We worked with hosts. We made mistakes. We figured out systems. We produced a lot of work. We helped other people make their shows while I kept carrying that original audio fiction idea around in the background.

Eventually, we made *Hellhound Country*, and that came close to the thing I had wanted from the beginning. It was audio fiction done professionally, with writing and actors and production and people who cared about making it good.

That mattered to me.

Not because it happened fast.

It did not.

It mattered because it proved something I already believed:

If you keep going long enough, the thing you meant to make has a way of circling back around.

But you have to keep going.

That is the part most people underestimate.

Starting is hard.

Keeping going is where the show is built.

## Your Story Is Not Too Ordinary

One of the lies people tell themselves is that their story is too ordinary.

They think they need some dramatic origin story. Some lightning bolt. Some giant life event that makes everybody lean forward and whisper, "Tell me more."

Maybe you have that.

Maybe you do not.

But a show does not always start with a lightning bolt.

Sometimes it starts with a question you cannot stop asking.

Sometimes it starts with a conversation you keep having.

Sometimes it starts with a thing you know that other people keep getting wrong.

Sometimes it starts with something funny that keeps happening in your world.

Sometimes it starts with grief.

Sometimes it starts with recovery.

Sometimes it starts with a job.

Sometimes it starts with a town.

Sometimes it starts with a hobby that became a weirdly large part of your personality.

Sometimes it starts with a stack of stories you have been carrying around for years.

Ordinary is not the problem.

Unexamined is the problem.

A lot of good shows come from looking at ordinary things long enough to notice what is actually there.

A family story.

A local business.

A high school football season.

A true crime case.

A classic movie.

A song.

A recipe.

A workplace lesson.

A mistake.

A friendship.

A weird little corner of history.

A personal obsession.

A show does not have to be about everything.

It has to be about something clearly enough that the right person recognizes it.

## You Are Not Too Late

Another lie:

"I am too late."

Too late because other people already started.

Too late because the space is crowded.

Too late because the technology moved fast.

Too late because younger people are already better at video.

Too late because the big shows are too big.

Too late because AI is changing everything.

Too late because the internet is loud.

Too late because you should have done this ten years ago.

Maybe you should have.

So what?

You did not.

Neither did I with about half the things I should have done earlier.

That is life.

The question is not whether starting earlier would have been better.

Of course it might have been.

The question is whether starting now still matters.

And it does.

The space is crowded, yes.

There are a lot of shows.

There are also a lot of restaurants, but people still get hungry.

There are a lot of books, but people still read.

There are a lot of songs, but people still find new ones that hit them at the right time.

There are a lot of movies, a lot of channels, a lot of creators, a lot of noise.

That does not mean there is no room.

It means the show has to know who it is for.

The world may not need another generic show.

It may need yours.

That is not ego.

That is specificity.

## The First Audience May Be Smaller Than You Want

This is where we need to be honest.

Your first audience may be small.

Very small.

Maybe painfully small.

Maybe "I think one of those downloads was me testing the link" small.

That does not mean the show is dead.

It means it is new.

A new show has not earned trust yet.

It has not earned routine.

It has not given people enough reasons to come back.

It has not built a trail.

It has not found its rhythm.

That takes time.

This is why I like the idea of finding your first ten people before you worry about the world. Kevin Kelly's "1,000 True Fans" idea and Seth Godin's "minimum viable audience" both point toward the same truth: a smaller group of people who actually care can matter more than a giant crowd that barely noticed you.

That applies perfectly here.

Do not start by asking, "How do I get everybody?"

Start by asking, "Who are the first ten people who might genuinely care?"

Then make something clear enough and useful enough that they would tell the eleventh.

That is how real growth starts.

Not always fast.

But real.

## AI Cannot Replace the Part That Matters

We are going to talk about AI later in this book because we have to.

AI is part of the world now.

It can help you brainstorm, outline, research, transcribe, summarize, write show notes, find clips, draft emails, organize ideas, clean up workflows, and get unstuck.

That is useful.

Very useful.

But AI cannot replace why your show should exist.

It cannot replace the moment you lived through.

It cannot replace your memory of the room.

It cannot replace the way you felt when the thing happened.

It cannot replace the joke your friend made.

It cannot replace the lesson you learned the hard way.

It cannot replace your taste.

It cannot replace your judgment.

It cannot replace the thing in your voice that tells the listener, "This person actually lived this."

AI is good at average.

You are not trying to be average.

You are trying to be specific.

Useful.

Recognizable.

Human.

AI can help carry the bricks.

It cannot decide why you are building the house.

That is still you.

## The Tools Are Finally Cheap Enough

Here is the good news.

It has never been easier to make a show.

That does not mean it is easy.

It means the gate is lower.

You do not need a radio station.

You do not need a television network.

You do not need a giant studio.

You do not need a truck full of equipment.

You do not need permission from some executive who thinks your idea needs to be "more broadly appealing," which usually means less interesting.

You can start with a simple microphone.

You can record at home.

You can use a phone or webcam for video.

You can publish through a hosting platform.

You can put video on YouTube.

You can build a simple website.

You can use AI to help with some of the boring or overwhelming parts.

You can create clips.

You can send emails.

You can reach people directly.

That is incredible.

But it also creates a problem.

When anything is possible, it becomes very easy to get overwhelmed.

So the job is not to do everything.

The job is to do the next right thing.

That is where this book is going.

Not everything.

The next right thing.

## Do Not Wait for Permission

Nobody is coming to give you permission.

I know that sounds harsh, but it is actually freeing.

Nobody is going to show up at your door and say, "We have reviewed your life, your experience, your emotional baggage, your available equipment, and your ability to speak clearly into a microphone, and we have decided you are now allowed to make a show."

That is not happening.

You decide.

You decide the idea matters enough to test.

You decide the audience is worth serving.

You decide the first version is allowed to be rough.

You decide the starter setup is good enough.

You decide to stop asking people who would never listen to the show whether they like the show.

You decide to make the thing.

That does not mean you ignore feedback.

It does not mean you refuse to learn.

It does not mean you pretend every idea is good just because it came from you.

It means you stop waiting for someone else to certify the beginning.

You are allowed to begin.

Right now.

With what you have.

Where you are.

As who you are.

## What Chapter 1 Is Asking From You

This chapter is not asking you to launch today.

It is not asking you to buy gear.

It is not asking you to announce anything.

It is not asking you to pick the final title or design the cover or start selling sponsors.

Not yet.

This chapter is asking you to admit one thing:

There is something here.

Maybe it is only a spark.

Maybe it is messy.

Maybe it is too big.

Maybe it is too vague.

Maybe it scares you.

Fine.

Write it down anyway.

In the companion workbook, there is a worksheet called **Why This Show Needs to Exist**.

Use it with this chapter.

Not because worksheets are magical. They are not. Half the time they just make you realize your handwriting has become a hostage note.

Use it because writing the idea down makes it harder for fear to keep it foggy.

Name the spark.

Name what you are carrying.

Name who might need it.

Name why it matters.

That is the first move.

Not the whole mountain.

The first move.

## Closing Thought

Your voice still matters.

Not because you are perfect.

Not because you are ready.

Not because you have all the answers.

Not because the world needs more noise.

Your voice matters because there are stories, lessons, questions, jokes, warnings, memories, and hard-earned truths that only sound right when they come from someone who has actually lived them.

That is enough to start.

The show does not have to be big yet.

It does not have to be polished yet.

It does not have to know everything it will become.

It just has to become real enough that you can work on it.

So start there.

Admit there is something here.

Then turn the page.

We will figure out what you are actually making next.

# Chapter 2: From Radio to RSS to AI

## How shows changed, why podcasting mattered, and why this moment belongs to people who remember the old one.

There is a funny thing about new media.

It is almost never as new as everybody says it is.

Every few years, somebody walks into the room waving a shiny new thing and says, "This changes everything."

And sometimes they are right.

But usually, it does not change everything all at once.

It changes the tools.

It changes the cost.

It changes who gets to make something.

It changes where the audience finds it.

It changes who gets paid.

It changes who gets ignored.

It changes what feels possible.

But the human stuff?

That stays weirdly stubborn.

People still want stories.

People still want voices they recognize.

People still want to laugh.

People still want to learn.

People still want to feel like somebody out there understands the thing they are going through.

People still want a reason to come back.

That was true with radio.

That was true with television.

That was true with cable.

That was true with MTV.

That was true with blogs.

That was true with podcasting.

That is true with YouTube.

And it is going to be true with AI.

The tools keep changing.

The reason people care stays human.

That is why I want to take a little detour here and look at how we got here.

Not because this book needs to become a history textbook. It does not. Nobody bought this book hoping to relive eighth-grade social studies with slightly better jokes.

But if you are Gen X, or close enough to Gen X that you remember when phones had cords and everybody knew at least one person with a waterbed, this history matters.

Because we did not just read about these media shifts.

We lived through a lot of them.

We grew up with old media.

We learned new media.

Now we are staring at AI media and trying to decide whether it is a tool, a threat, a shortcut, a mess, a miracle, or some combination of all five.

And here is my take:

We are not behind.

We are the bridge.

We remember what shows felt like before everything became "content."

That matters more than people think.

## Radio: The First Voice in the Room

Before television took over the living room, radio owned the imagination.

Radio did not have pictures, so it had to build them in your head.

That is powerful.

A voice came through a box, and suddenly a family could hear music, news, comedy, drama, sports, sermons, farm reports, weather, mysteries, war updates, fireside chats, baseball games, advertisements, and voices from places they would never visit.

Think about how strange that must have felt at first.

A voice in the house that did not belong to anyone in the house.

That is still kind of magic.

In 1920, KDKA in Pittsburgh broadcast presidential election returns, and that moment is often described as the beginning of commercial radio broadcasting in the United States. What is interesting is not just that the station existed. It is why the whole system made sense.

Radios needed something to play.

Broadcasters needed people with radios.

The device needed content.

The content made the device worth buying.

That pattern keeps repeating.

A new technology shows up.

At first, people talk about the technology.

Then somebody has to make something worth using it for.

That is where creators come in.

A microphone by itself is nothing.

A radio tower by itself is nothing.

An RSS feed by itself is nothing.

A YouTube channel by itself is nothing.

An AI tool by itself is nothing.

The question is always:

What are we going to make with it?

## Radio Taught Us Companionship

Radio understood something that every show creator should understand.

A voice can become company.

People did not only listen to radio for information.

They listened because the voices became part of life.

Morning shows.

Late-night DJs.

Sports announcers.

Local news.

Call-in shows.

Talk radio.

Weather reports.

Commercial jingles that got stuck in your head against your will and probably still live there rent-free.

Radio became ritual.

It was in the kitchen.

In the car.

In the garage.

At work.

At night.

In the background.

And sometimes right in the foreground, when something mattered.

That is one of the reasons podcasting eventually worked so well. It took that intimacy and made it portable, personal, and on-demand.

But the emotional idea was already there.

A voice can become a habit.

A host can become familiar.

A show can become part of someone's routine.

If you are making a show now, do not underestimate that.

You may be thinking about downloads, clips, thumbnails, and sponsors.

Fine.

Those matter.

But part of the power is still ancient in media terms:

A person hears you enough times, and you start becoming familiar.

Familiar becomes trusted.

Trusted becomes valuable.

## Television: The Living Room Gets a Window

Then television moved in.

Radio had asked people to imagine the picture.

Television gave them the picture.

That changed the whole relationship.

Now the host had a face.

The set mattered.

The clothes mattered.

The timing mattered.

The camera mattered.

A show had a look.

A show had a theme song.

A show had a schedule.

A show had a place in the week.

We grew up understanding this without thinking about it.

A sitcom felt different from a police drama.

A game show felt different from the evening news.

A Saturday morning cartoon felt different from a late-night talk show.

A football pregame show felt different from a soap opera.

You did not need someone to explain the format. You felt it.

That is one of the biggest advantages people our age may have.

We grew up with formats.

We understood shows as things with shape.

Openings.

Segments.

Commercial breaks.

Cliffhangers.

Catchphrases.

Theme music.

Credits.

Reruns.

Special episodes.

Finales.

All of that taught us that a show is more than information.

A show is an experience.

That matters now because a lot of people making digital content forget to make an experience.

They upload.

They post.

They clip.

They react.

They feed the machine.

But they do not always build a show.

And that is where people with older media instincts can do something interesting.

We can take the old idea of a show and use the new tools to make it ourselves.

## Cable: More Channels, More Niches

For a long time, television felt limited.

A few networks.

A few choices.

Everybody watching a lot of the same things.

Then cable changed the shelf space.

Suddenly there were channels for music, sports, news, movies, weather, kids, comedy, education, shopping, religion, and whatever strange thing you found after midnight and never fully understood.

Cable did something important.

It made niche feel normal.

You did not need one channel to serve everybody.

You could have ESPN for sports.

CNN for news.

Nickelodeon for kids.

MTV for music.

The Weather Channel for people who apparently wanted vibes with a five-day forecast.

And on and on.

That shift matters because podcasting later took the niche idea and blew it wide open.

Cable said, "There can be more channels."

Podcasting said, "There can be a channel for almost anything."

You like a specific TV show?

There is a podcast.

You like a specific team?

There is a podcast.

You like a specific kind of history, horror, business, parenting, faith, comedy, conspiracy, science, recovery, or weird local story?

There is probably a podcast.

And if there is not, that might be your opening.

The lesson from cable is not just that more choices appeared.

The lesson is that people like finding a place that feels made for them.

That is the niche advantage.

Not everybody.

Somebody.

## MTV: Short-Form Was Already Teaching Us

If you are Gen X, MTV did something to your brain.

I do not mean that medically, though maybe.

I mean creatively.

When MTV launched in 1981, it took music and turned it into a visual identity machine. A song was no longer just something you heard. It became something you saw. The clothes, the lighting, the editing, the attitude, the set, the camera movement, the weird smoke machine that apparently came standard with every video in the eighties — all of it became part of the message.

Music videos were short-form storytelling.

They were mood.

They were hooks.

They were branding.

They were performance.

They were style.

They were sometimes nonsense, but confident nonsense, which is its own art form.

And they taught us something.

A few minutes can build a world.

A strong visual can make a song unforgettable.

A hook matters.

A first impression matters.

A vibe matters.

Packaging matters.

That is not far from what clips do now.

People talk about short-form video like it appeared out of nowhere because somebody invented vertical scrolling.

No.

Short-form has been shaping us for decades.

Commercials were short-form.

Movie trailers were short-form.

Music videos were short-form.

Sitcom cold opens were short-form.

Saturday Night Live sketches were short-form.

The difference now is distribution.

Instead of waiting for a network, a record label, or a cable channel, you can make the moment and publish it yourself.

That is the shift.

The MTV lesson for show creators is simple:

Do not think clips are just leftovers.

A good clip has a hook, a mood, and a reason to exist.

But also remember this:

The clip should point back to something.

A music video pointed back to the song, the album, the artist, the identity.

Your clip should point back to the show.

If the clip gets attention but nobody understands what the show is, that is noise.

Make the moment.

But build the show.

## Home Video and Public Access: The Gate Cracks Open

Before the internet made everyone a publisher, video cameras and public access cracked the door open a little.

Camcorders let families record birthdays, school plays, Little League games, vacations, weddings, and hours of footage where someone forgot the camera was still on and filmed the floor.

Public access let regular people get on local television.

Was it always good?

No.

Absolutely not.

Some of it was rough.

Some of it was strange.

Some of it looked like it had a production budget of eleven dollars and a sandwich.

But that was also part of the beauty.

It proved something.

Not every show had to come from a network.

Not every voice had to be polished.

Not every idea needed permission from a corporate office.

People could make things.

Imperfect things.

Local things.

Odd things.

Personal things.

That spirit matters.

Because the internet did not invent the desire to create outside the gate.

It just made the gate easier to walk around.

## The Internet: Everybody Gets a Printing Press, Then a Radio Station, Then a TV Channel

The early internet felt like a mess because it was a mess.

But it was an exciting mess.

Websites.

Forums.

Email lists.

Message boards.

Blogs.

AIM away messages that were somehow both poetry and a cry for help.

People started publishing without asking permission.

That was a big deal.

Before that, if you wanted to reach people, you usually needed access to someone else's system.

A newspaper.

A radio station.

A television station.

A publisher.

A record label.

A distributor.

The web changed that.

Now a person could write something and publish it.

Not always well.

Not always beautifully.

But directly.

Blogs especially mattered because they brought back voice.

Not institutional voice.

Personal voice.

A person thinking out loud.

A person linking to things.

A person building an audience through consistency, point of view, and usefulness.

That matters because podcasting came out of that world.

Podcasting was not born fully formed as a giant industry.

It came out of blogging, RSS, MP3s, portable players, and people wanting to send audio directly to others without needing a radio station.

It was weird at first.

Most good things are.

## RSS: The Boring Pipe That Changed Everything

RSS is not exciting to talk about.

It sounds like something printed on the back of a router.

But RSS helped make podcasting possible.

RSS allowed people to subscribe to updates from websites and blogs. Then developers figured out how to attach media files to those feeds using enclosures.

That meant audio could travel through a subscription feed.

A person could publish an audio file.

A listener could subscribe.

New episodes could arrive automatically.

That was the magic.

Not just that audio existed online.

Audio had existed online before.

The magic was subscription and delivery.

The listener did not have to keep checking a website.

The show came to them.

That is the difference between a random file and a show relationship.

If radio was live and scheduled, podcasting became automatic and personal.

Radio said:

"Be here at this time."

Podcasting said:

"I will be waiting when you are ready."

That is a huge shift.

Especially for busy people.

Especially for commuters.

Especially for people who wanted control.

Especially for people who had grown tired of whatever the radio station decided to give them.

## The iPod Moment

The word podcast itself comes from that era.

iPod plus broadcast.

A strange little mashup that somehow stuck.

In 2004, the term podcast started appearing to describe downloadable audio delivered through RSS subscription technology. In 2005, Apple built podcast discovery and subscription into iTunes, and that helped move podcasting from a geeky early-adopter space toward the mainstream.

That mattered.

Because technology adoption often needs a bridge.

The idea may already exist.

The tools may already exist.

The passionate nerds may already be doing it.

But most people need the process to get easier.

Apple made it easier for regular listeners to find, subscribe, and listen.

That helped podcasting grow.

This is another pattern that repeats.

A medium may be technically possible for years before it becomes culturally normal.

AI is in a similar moment now.

The tools exist.

The early adopters are everywhere.

The hype is loud.

The actual useful workflows are still being sorted out.

That is normal.

The question is not, "Is the tool new?"

The question is, "Has the tool become easy and useful enough for normal people to build with it?"

Podcasting crossed that line when subscription and listening got easier.

AI is crossing that line now.

## Podcasting: Radio Without the Station

Podcasting did something beautiful.

It let people make radio without owning a radio station.

That is not technically perfect, but emotionally it is right.

A person could talk about something specific, upload it, and reach people who cared.

No program director.

No broadcast license.

No tower.

No local signal.

No one saying, "This is too niche."

That changed everything.

The weirdest part is that the niche became the strength.

Traditional broadcasting had to care about large audiences because airtime was limited.

Podcasting did not have the same shelf-space problem.

You could make a show about one team, one crime, one hobby, one town, one profession, one fandom, one belief system, one kind of story, one personality, one obsession.

The internet made room for the long tail.

And podcasting filled it with voices.

Some shows were polished.

Some were rough.

Some sounded like they were recorded in a closet because they were recorded in a closet.

Some became huge.

Most did not.

But the gate had changed.

That is the important part.

A show could start small and still matter.

## The Smartphone: The Studio and the Audience Move Into Your Pocket

Then the smartphone changed the whole thing again.

The phone became a recorder, camera, editor, publishing device, listening device, viewing device, map, notebook, calendar, flashlight, and emotional support rectangle.

This is where media creation and media consumption collapsed into the same object.

You could record on the same device where someone else would listen.

You could shoot a video on the same device where someone else would watch.

You could publish from the same device where someone else would comment.

That changed the speed.

It also changed expectations.

People started expecting media to be available everywhere.

In the car.

In bed.

At work.

At lunch.

On the toilet.

Yes, the toilet.

Let's not pretend.

The phone made everything portable and private.

That helped podcasting.

It helped video.

It helped social media.

It helped short-form.

It also made attention harder to earn because now your show is competing with everything.

Not just other shows.

Text messages.

Games.

Sports scores.

Breaking news.

Family group chats.

Emails.

Shopping apps.

Weather alerts.

That one app you opened for thirty seconds and somehow lost twenty minutes.

This is the world your show enters.

So the show has to be clear.

It has to be worth returning to.

It has to respect time.

Because attention is no longer sitting politely in a living room waiting for your program to begin.

Attention is running through traffic with earbuds in.

## YouTube: Everybody Gets a TV Channel

YouTube changed the creator world because it made video publishing feel possible for regular people.

At first, a lot of it was rough.

That was part of the charm.

Home videos.

Skateboard clips.

Bedroom rants.

Tutorials.

Comedy sketches.

Music.

Weird little videos people emailed each other before social media swallowed everything.

Then it grew up.

Creators built channels.

Channels became shows.

Shows became businesses.

Video became searchable, shareable, recommended, monetized, and global.

That changed expectations again.

Now people could watch people like them.

Not only celebrities.

Not only network hosts.

Not only polished broadcasters.

Regular people with knowledge, charisma, obsession, humor, or a useful skill could build an audience.

YouTube also trained audiences to search for answers in video.

How do I fix this sink?

How do I use this software?

What microphone should I buy?

What happened in this case?

Is this movie worth watching?

Why is my car making that noise?

Somewhere along the way, YouTube became part television, part search engine, part community, part school, part rabbit hole, and part time machine.

For show creators, that matters.

If you are making a show now, video is not mandatory, but video is part of the ecosystem.

You do not have to become a YouTuber in the fake exaggerated sense.

But you should understand that many people now discover shows by watching.

That is the world.

## Social Media: The Feed Takes Over

Then the feed became the dominant media experience.

Facebook.

Twitter.

Instagram.

TikTok.

LinkedIn.

Whatever else is fighting for our souls this week.

The feed changed how people found things.

Instead of choosing a show first, people started encountering moments.

A clip.

A quote.

A post.

A reaction.

A headline.

A thumbnail.

A friend's share.

The feed made discovery faster and messier.

It also made creators feel like they had to be everywhere all the time.

That is exhausting.

And for many people, especially older creators who did not grow up performing online, it can feel unnatural.

The feed rewards frequency, novelty, emotion, conflict, speed, and sometimes nonsense.

That does not mean you should ignore it.

It means you should use it without letting it become the boss.

Your show needs identity beyond the feed.

A clip may introduce someone to you.

A post may remind them.

A share may bring them in.

But the show has to give them somewhere to land.

Otherwise, you are just tossing moments into a river.

## Streaming: Everything Becomes On-Demand

Streaming changed patience.

That is one of the biggest shifts.

We used to wait.

Wait for the show to come on.

Wait through commercials.

Wait for next week.

Wait for the rerun.

Wait for the tape to rewind.

Wait for the video store to have a copy.

Now everything is there.

Whole seasons.

Whole catalogs.

Whole channels.

Whole archives.

That changed audience expectations.

People still follow schedules, especially for sports, news, live events, and community shows. But they also expect to access things when they want them.

That means your show needs to be organized.

If someone finds you on episode forty-seven, can they understand what the show is?

Can they find the best starter episodes?

Can they go back?

Can they binge a season?

Can they follow a topic?

Can they watch or listen on their schedule?

On-demand is powerful, but it also puts more responsibility on the creator.

You are not only making the next episode.

You are building an archive.

That archive should be usable.

## AI: The Next Tool Walks Into the Room

And now AI is here.

AI is different because it does not just distribute media.

It helps make it.

That is why people are reacting so strongly.

Radio changed reach.

Television changed visual storytelling.

Cable changed niche channels.

The internet changed publishing.

RSS changed subscription delivery.

Smartphones changed access and creation.

YouTube changed video distribution.

Social media changed discovery.

AI changes production, research, packaging, search, and maybe eventually the way audiences find and evaluate shows.

That is a big deal.

AI can help you brainstorm episode ideas.

It can help outline.

It can help research.

It can summarize transcripts.

It can suggest clips.

It can write show notes.

It can draft guest emails.

It can help build sponsor copy.

It can clean up audio.

It can generate images.

It can help edit video.

It can translate.

It can help repurpose one episode into many pieces.

That is useful.

It is also dangerous if used lazily.

Because AI is very good at average.

It can make everything sound smoother and less alive.

It can give you the same advice it gives everybody else.

It can flatten your voice.

It can generate confident nonsense.

It can make fake things look real enough to confuse people.

It can make creators feel like they are producing more while actually saying less.

So the AI question is not:

Can I use it?

Of course you can.

The better question is:

Where can AI reduce friction without removing the human reason the show exists?

That is the line.

Use AI to carry weight.

Do not let it carry the meaning.

## The Future: Search Becomes Conversation

Search is changing too.

For years, we thought about search as typing words into a box and getting links.

That still matters.

But AI search and answer engines are making search more conversational.

People ask full questions.

Tools summarize.

Answers appear before links.

Recommendations may come through AI assistants instead of only search pages.

That means your show has to be understandable not only to humans but to systems trying to summarize the web.

But here is the key:

The way to prepare is not to become robotic.

The way to prepare is to become clearer.

Clear titles.

Useful episode pages.

Transcripts.

Show notes.

Topic pages.

Guest pages.

Real examples.

Original experience.

Human voice.

If AI tools are going to summarize the world, then the best defense is having something specific enough to be worth summarizing and clear enough to be found.

Do not hide everything inside an audio file.

Do not make every episode title a private joke.

Do not publish without context.

Do not assume the platforms will explain you.

Make the trail.

The future of discovery may be more automated, but the need for clarity is going up, not down.

## The Future: Trust Becomes More Valuable

As AI makes it easier to generate words, images, voices, and videos, trust is going to become more valuable.

Maybe much more valuable.

If anyone can generate a smooth explanation, who do you trust?

If anyone can create a fake voice, who do you believe?

If anyone can make a fake image, what feels real?

If anyone can generate a thousand articles, what is worth reading?

The answer is not polish.

The answer is trust.

A known voice.

A real person.

A consistent show.

A clear point of view.

A history of being useful.

A relationship with the audience.

A willingness to correct mistakes.

A human being who can say, "Here is what I actually think, here is what I actually saw, here is what I actually tried, here is what I actually learned."

That is going to matter.

This is why I do not think older creators should panic about AI.

I think they should learn it.

Use it.

Understand it.

But do not compete with AI by trying to become faster and more generic.

That is a losing game.

Compete by being more human.

More specific.

More trusted.

More experienced.

More useful.

More yourself.

AI can make average content cheap.

So do not make average content.

## The Future: The Gatekeepers Keep Moving

Every media shift changes the gatekeepers.

Radio had station owners and regulators.

Television had networks.

Cable had channel space.

Publishing had editors and distributors.

Music had labels.

Podcasting lowered the gate, but platforms and charts still mattered.

YouTube lowered the gate, but algorithms became new gatekeepers.

Social media lowered the gate, then made the feed the gatekeeper.

AI may lower some gates and create new ones.

Maybe AI tools recommend shows.

Maybe answer engines quote certain sources.

Maybe platforms favor certain formats.

Maybe synthetic media floods the zone.

Maybe trust badges, human verification, and provenance matter more.

Maybe small creators get new power.

Maybe large platforms absorb even more attention.

Probably some of all of it.

That is how these things go.

Do not build your whole creative life around one gatekeeper.

Build around the show.

Build around the audience.

Build around the home base.

Build around trust.

Build around a direct relationship where you can.

Platforms change.

Formats shift.

Algorithms wobble around like shopping carts with one bad wheel.

But a trusted show with a clear audience can move.

It can be audio.

It can be video.

It can become a newsletter.

It can become a book.

It can become a live event.

It can become a course.

It can become a community.

It can become a documentary.

It can become something you cannot see yet.

The show is the portable part.

## Why This Moment Belongs to People Who Remember the Old One

This is the part I really care about.

A lot of people who remember the old media world think the new one is not for them.

They are wrong.

They may not like every part of it.

I do not either.

Some of it is annoying.

Some of it is shallow.

Some of it feels like every platform is trying to turn human attention into a slot machine.

But the tools themselves are not the enemy.

The tools are tools.

And people with lived experience can use them.

In fact, this may be one of the best times ever for people with stories, memory, and perspective.

Because the cost of making a show is lower.

The tools are easier.

The gatekeepers are fewer.

The audience can be niche.

The archive can live forever.

AI can help with the boring parts.

Video can help people see you.

Audio can still build intimacy.

Email can still build direct connection.

Websites can still give the show a home.

You do not have to become somebody else.

You do not have to pretend to be young.

You do not have to chase every trend.

You can take what you learned from radio, television, cable, MTV, video stores, newspapers, magazines, blogs, podcasts, and life, and build a show that uses the new tools without losing the old soul.

That is the opportunity.

Not nostalgia.

Translation.

You are translating experience into a modern format.

That is valuable.

## What This Means for Your Show

So what does all this history mean for you?

It means you are part of a long line of people using new tools to do an old human thing.

Talk.

Tell stories.

Teach.

Entertain.

Warn.

Remember.

Argue.

Comfort.

Connect.

It means the technology will keep changing, so do not wait for it to settle down.

It will not.

It means the show matters more than the platform.

It means clarity matters because discovery is getting more complicated.

It means trust matters because synthetic media is going to make people more suspicious.

It means your lived experience is not a liability.

It is the reason the show might matter.

It means you should use AI, but not disappear into it.

It means you should understand video, but not let video kill the show.

It means you should use clips, but not mistake clips for the whole thing.

It means you should build a home base, because rented land keeps changing the rent.

It means you should stop asking whether you are too late.

You are not.

You are standing in the middle of another media shift.

You have seen those before.

You made it through dial-up.

You made it through programming a VCR, or at least pretending you knew how.

You made it through MySpace profile songs.

You made it through people saying “the information superhighway” with a straight face.

You can make it through this.

## Closing Thought

From radio to RSS to AI, the story is not just about technology.

It is about access.

Who gets to speak?

Who gets to publish?

Who gets to be heard?

Who gets to build something without asking permission?

Every shift opens doors and creates new problems.

Radio brought voices into homes.

Television gave those voices faces.

Cable made room for niches.

MTV taught us the power of short-form visual identity.

The internet gave people publishing tools.

RSS made subscription audio possible.

Podcasting let regular people make radio without a station.

YouTube gave regular people something like a TV channel.

Social media made discovery fast and chaotic.

AI is giving creators a production assistant, a research helper, a packaging tool, and a new set of ethical headaches.

And through all of it, the human need stays.

People still want a good show.

So make one.

Use the tools.

Learn the history.

Respect the audience.

Keep your voice.

The future is not asking you to become fake.

It is asking you to become clear.

And maybe, if we do this right, the next era of shows will not belong only to the loudest, youngest, fastest, or most algorithm-friendly.

Maybe it will also belong to the people who remember what a show is supposed to feel like.

That sounds like us.

Let's not waste it.

# Chapter 3: What Are You Actually Making?

Before you buy a microphone, before you open Canva, before you register a domain, before you start arguing with yourself about whether the show should be audio, video, or both, you need to answer one question.

What are you actually making?

Not, "I want to start a podcast." That is not enough. That is like saying, "I want to open a restaurant," but you do not know whether it is barbecue, tacos, breakfast, fine dining, a food truck, or a weird little place that only serves soup and pie.

A show is not just a recording. A show is a promise.

You are promising a listener or viewer that if they give you their time, you are going to give them something back. Maybe it is information. Maybe it is entertainment. Maybe it is companionship. Maybe it is a story. Maybe it is a laugh. Maybe it is a feeling that somebody else out there sees the world the way they do.

But there has to be a promise.

A lot of people skip this part because it feels easier to shop. Shopping feels productive. Looking at microphones feels productive. Watching studio tours feels productive. Comparing hosting platforms feels productive. Designing artwork feels productive. Reading about cameras and lights and AI editing tools feels productive.

And some of that stuff matters.

Eventually.

But early on, a lot of it is just fancy procrastination. The real work is figuring out the show.

## Have the First Pre-Production Meeting With Yourself

At Rogue, when we start working on a show, we usually have some kind of pre-production conversation. Sometimes it is formal. Sometimes it is loose. But one way or another, we need to know what we are making.

What is the show about? Who is the host? Who is it for? What should it feel like? Is it funny? Serious? Helpful? Weird? Local? Personal? Educational? Investigative? Comforting? Loud? Quiet? Opinionated? Story-driven?

What does the listener get from it?

Why would somebody come back for episode two?

These are not little questions. These are the show.

And there is no reason you cannot have that meeting with yourself. In fact, you should. Sit down with a notebook, a document, a voice memo, a cup of coffee, whatever works, and ask yourself the questions somebody else would ask if they were helping you build this from scratch.

Do not start by asking, "What gear do I need?"

Start by asking, "Why does this show need to exist?"

That sounds dramatic, but it matters. Because if you do not know why the show exists, you will start copying whatever you think a show is supposed to sound like. You will make a generic interview show. Or a generic advice show. Or a generic commentary show. Or a generic "me and my buddy talk about stuff" show.

There is nothing wrong with any of those formats if there is a clear reason behind them.

But "we talk about stuff" is not a show. It is a conversation looking for a spine.

## The One-Sentence Test

Here is one of the simplest tests you can give your idea.

Can you explain your show in one sentence?

Not a paragraph. Not a rambling explanation. Not "well, it is kind of about..."

One sentence.

"This is a weekly show where two longtime high school football coaches tell the stories behind Texas small-town football."

That makes sense.

"This is a show where I interview local business owners about how they survived, changed, and kept going."

That makes sense.

"This is an audio fiction series about a late-night radio host in West Texas who starts receiving calls from people who may not be alive."

That makes sense.

The sentence does not have to be perfect. It can change. It probably will change. But if you cannot explain the show simply, your future listener probably cannot explain it either. And if they cannot explain it, they probably will not share it.

## Who Is This For?

A lot of new creators say, "It is for everybody."

No, it is not.

And that is good news.

You do not need everybody. You need the right people. "Everybody" is not an audience. A specific person is an audience.

If your show is about parenting adult children, that is not for everybody. If your show is about horror movies from the VHS era, that is not for everybody. If your show is about starting over after fifty, that is not for everybody. If your show is about local restaurants, minor league baseball, true crime in Texas, grief, addiction recovery, classic country music, AI tools for small business owners, or weird roadside attractions, that is not for everybody.

Good.

The more clearly you can picture the listener, the easier your decisions become. Should the show be funny or serious? Depends on the listener. Should it be thirty minutes or ninety minutes? Depends on the listener. Should it be audio, video, or both? Depends on the listener. Should it be on Facebook, LinkedIn, YouTube, Instagram, TikTok, or none of those at first? Depends on the listener.

When you know who you are talking to, you stop shouting into the wind.

## Why Should They Care?

This is the question that hurts a little.

Why should they care?

Not why do you care. Why should they care?

That does not mean your passion is unimportant. Your passion is fuel. But the listener is not required to care just because you care. You have to give them a reason.

Maybe you know something they need to know. Maybe you have lived through something they are living through now. Maybe you can make a complicated topic feel simple. Maybe you can make them laugh during a hard week. Maybe you can tell stories nobody else is telling. Maybe you can give them a place to belong. Maybe you can help them feel less alone.

That is where the show starts to matter.

A show grows when the creator's reason for making it overlaps with the audience's reason for needing it. That overlap is the sweet spot.

## Pick a Format You Can Actually Survive

Once the idea is clearer, then you can start thinking about format.

You can make an interview show. You can make a solo show. You can make a co-hosted show. You can make a documentary series. You can make audio fiction. You can make a business show. You can make a comedy show. You can make a video show. You can make short-form clips that lead into a longer show.

But do not pick the format just because it sounds impressive. Pick the format you can actually survive.

Interview shows are easy to start, but they depend on booking guests. Solo shows give you control, but they require preparation. Co-hosted shows can be great if the chemistry is real, but scheduling and balance can become problems. Documentary shows can be powerful, but research and editing take time. Audio fiction is beautiful, but it is not casual. It needs writing, voices, sound design, pacing, and patience. Video shows can help people connect with you, but video adds work.

The best format is not the fanciest one. The best format is the one you can keep making when life gets busy.

## The Ten-Episode Test

Before you launch, write down ten episode ideas.

Not one. Not three. Ten.

If you cannot come up with ten possible episodes, the idea may not be ready yet. That does not mean it is bad. It means it needs more shape.

The first ten do not have to be final titles. They can be rough. But they should prove the show has legs. If your show is an interview show, list ten guests or guest types. If it is a solo show, list ten topics. If it is documentary, list ten story beats or possible episodes. If it is audio fiction, list the first ten scenes, chapters, or installments. If it is educational, list ten problems you can help solve.

This tells you whether the idea has depth, and it also makes starting easier. One of the reasons people quit is that every episode feels like starting from scratch. Do not do that to yourself. Build the idea bank early.

## The Show Is Not the Topic

This is where a lot of people get tangled up.

They think the topic is the show.

It is not.

The topic is what you talk about.

The show is how you deliver the promise.

Two shows can have the exact same topic and be completely different.

Take movies.

One show might be two friends arguing about old action movies like they are solving international diplomacy.

Another might be a serious film-history show.

Another might be a parent and adult child watching the movies one of them grew up with.

Another might be a show about how movies shaped Gen X expectations of work, romance, violence, friendship, and whether every problem could be solved by one guy in a leather jacket.

Same topic.

Different show.

That is why "my show is about movies" is not enough.

What is the angle?

Who is talking?

Who is listening?

What does the listener get?

Why this show and not the thousand other movie shows already out there?

This is not meant to scare you. It is meant to free you.

You do not need to invent a topic nobody has ever touched.

Good luck with that. The internet has touched everything. It has touched things that should have been left alone.

You need your angle.

Your point of view.

Your reason.

Your promise.

That is what makes it a show.

## The Promise Should Be Repeatable

The show promise should be something you can keep episode after episode.

If the promise is too vague, you will drift.

If the promise is too big, you will drown.

If the promise is too narrow, you will run out of road.

A good promise has room to move, but it still tells the audience what kind of ride they are on.

Here are a few examples.

Weak promise:

"We talk about life."

That is not a promise. That is what happens when two people sit on a porch long enough.

Better promise:

"Every week, we talk with people who rebuilt their lives after fifty and pull out the practical decisions that helped them start over."

Now we know the audience, the format, the emotional territory, and the value.

Weak promise:

"We cover technology."

That is a planet, not a show.

Better promise:

"We explain new technology and AI tools to people who remember life before Wi-Fi and do not want to feel stupid asking basic questions."

Now there is a voice. There is a person in mind. There is a real need.

Weak promise:

"We tell local stories."

Better promise:

"We tell the stories behind the people, places, businesses, and legends that shaped Waco before the internet flattened everything into the same five coffee shop aesthetics."

That has a world.

That has a point of view.

You do not need the sentence to be perfect on day one. But you do need something solid enough that you can make decisions with it.

## The Audience Is Not a Demographic Only

A demographic can help.

Age, location, income, gender, profession, and interests can matter.

But a demographic is not the whole person.

"Men 45 to 64" is not an audience. It is a spreadsheet row.

"People over forty-five who have stories, skills, and opinions but feel like the creator economy passed them by" is closer.

"Local business owners who know they need to show up online but hate sounding like everyone else" is closer.

"Parents whose kids are grown and who are trying to figure out who they are now" is closer.

"Sports fans who want real conversation instead of hot-take theater" is closer.

Think in terms of situation.

What is happening in this person's life?

What are they trying to do?

What are they tired of?

What do they secretly wish someone would explain?

What do they feel embarrassed about not knowing?

What do they love enough to spend time on?

What kind of host would they trust?

That is more useful than saying, "My audience is adults."

Congratulations. So is the audience for lawn chairs.

Get more specific.

## The Anti-Audience

It also helps to know who the show is not for.

This does not have to be mean.

You are not building a list of enemies. Though, if that helps you creatively, write it privately and do not put it on the website like a lunatic.

The anti-audience is the group you do not need to please.

If your show is for beginners, it does not need to impress experts every week.

If your show is for Gen X and older creators, it does not need to chase every trend aimed at teenagers.

If your show is slow, thoughtful, and story-driven, it does not need to satisfy people who only want thirty-second summaries.

If your show is local, it does not need to pretend to be national on day one.

If your show is funny and loose, it does not need to satisfy people who want a formal lecture.

Knowing who it is not for gives you permission to stop sanding off the edges.

That matters.

The edges are often where the connection happens.

## What Kind of Return Are You Offering?

Every listener is making a trade.

They give time.

You give something back.

So what are you giving?

Information?

Entertainment?

A sense of belonging?

A useful framework?

A story they will remember?

A laugh?

A practical next step?

A place where they can feel understood?

A little company while they drive?

There is no one right answer.

But you need an answer.

A true crime show may offer suspense, investigation, empathy, and resolution.

A business show may offer practical insight and confidence.

A comedy show may offer escape.

A local history show may offer connection to place.

An audio fiction show may offer transportation to another world.

A creator show may offer courage and a system.

This book is built around that last one.

If someone reads it, I want them to feel less overwhelmed, more equipped, and more willing to make the first version.

That is the return.

Your show needs one too.

## The Napkin Version

Before you overbuild anything, write the napkin version of the show.

Not the polished pitch.

Not the sponsor deck.

Not the website copy.

The messy version you would say to a friend.

Something like:

"I want to make a show for people our age who have stories and ideas but feel like podcasting, YouTube, and AI are all moving too fast. I want to help them make real shows without pretending they are twenty-five or turning into some fake influencer."

That is a show seed.

Or:

"I want to talk to people in our town who built things, lost things, survived things, and remember what this place used to be before everything became a chain restaurant and a parking lot."

That is a show seed.

Or:

"I want to make spooky audio stories that feel like old radio, late-night TV, and the kind of thing you found on cable when you should have been asleep."

That is a show seed.

Write that first.

Make it human.

Then clean it up.

## How You Know the Idea Is Getting Clearer

You know the idea is getting clearer when decisions become easier.

Should this guest be on?

Does the promise support them?

Should this episode be ninety minutes?

Does the listener need that?

Should we post on LinkedIn?

Is the audience there?

Should the show be funny?

Would that make the promise stronger?

Should we add video?

Does it serve the show or only our insecurity?

Clarity is not just for marketing.

Clarity is a decision-making tool.

When the show is clear, you stop asking, "What would a podcast do?"

You ask, "What would this show do?"

That is a much better question.

## A Few Starting Formats That Work

Here are some first-season formats that can work without getting too heavy.

**The Ten-Question Interview**

Every guest answers a similar set of core questions, with room for follow-up. This gives structure without killing the conversation.

**The One-Problem Episode**

Each episode solves or explores one specific problem. Good for teaching, business, coaching, health, technology, or creator shows.

**The Story Plus Lesson**

Start with a story, then pull out what it means. Good for personal, faith, recovery, career, or second-act shows.

**The Roundtable**

A small recurring group talks through a specific topic. Good for sports, movies, local issues, pop culture, or opinion shows.

**The Season Arc**

One larger theme broken into episodes. Good for documentary, fiction, history, true crime, or a guided learning series.

**The Field Trip**

The show visits places, people, events, or local stories. Good for local history, food, travel, community, and nostalgia.

The format is not the cage.

It is the track.

It lets the train move.

Without it, you are just pushing a heavy thing across a field.

## When the Show Changes

Here is a relief: the show can change.

It probably will.

The first version may be too broad.

The second version may be too serious.

The third version may find the humor.

The fourth version may reveal that the best part is the listener questions.

The fifth version may show that your co-host chemistry is the real engine.

The sixth version may prove the episodes should be shorter.

That is development.

That is not failure.

But you need a starting version so you have something to learn from.

You cannot evolve a show that does not exist.

That is why the first clear promise matters.

Not because it is final.

Because it gives you a place to begin.

## Closing Thought

Your first job is not to buy the right microphone. Your first job is to know what you are trying to say, who you are saying it to, and why it matters.

The gear comes later. The name comes later. The artwork comes later. The platforms come later.

First, figure out the show.

Not perfectly.

Just clearly enough to start.

# Chapter 4: Pick Your Lane Before You Hit Record

## Solo, interview, co-hosted, documentary, fiction, local, business, hybrid, and how to choose the show you can actually make.

There is a moment in every show idea where you have to stop admiring the idea and start making decisions.

That is the part people avoid.

Because in the idea stage, everything is possible.

Your show can be funny and serious.

Short and long.

Audio and video.

Interview and solo.

Local and national.

Educational and entertaining.

A business tool and a creative outlet.

A weekly show and a seasonal show.

A YouTube channel and a podcast and a newsletter and a live event and maybe a book and a documentary and, if we are being honest, probably a T-shirt you do not need yet.

The idea stage is fun because the show has no limits.

The production stage has limits.

Time.

Money.

Energy.

Skill.

Equipment.

Guests.

Editing.

Your family.

Your job.

Your tolerance for hearing your own voice.

That drawer full of old cables that somehow still owns part of your soul.

At some point, you have to pick a lane.

Not forever.

Not for the rest of your life.

Not carved into stone and carried down from the mountain while everyone waits quietly.

Just a lane.

A starting lane.

A first-season lane.

A first-ten-episodes lane.

Because a show without a lane usually becomes a mess.

And not a fun mess.

Not a "cool record store in 1993" mess.

More like a "garage after a birthday party and a failed home repair project" mess.

A show can evolve.

It can grow.

It can change format.

It can add video.

It can bring in guests.

It can become seasonal.

It can become live.

It can become something bigger than you expected.

But it needs a starting shape.

That is what this chapter is about.

Not killing your creativity.

Giving it a road.

## The Lane Is Not the Prison

Let's get one fear out of the way.

Picking a lane does not mean trapping yourself.

People resist choosing because they think every choice eliminates the future.

If I start solo, can I never have guests?

If I start audio-only, can I never do video?

If I start local, can I never go broader?

If I make a business show, can it never be personal?

If I make a comedy show, can it never get serious?

Of course not.

Shows are allowed to grow up.

But they have to start somewhere.

Think of a lane like a bowling lane.

Yes, that is where we are going with this.

You throw the ball down the lane. The lane gives the ball direction. Without the lane, you are just rolling a heavy object across a room and hoping nobody gets hurt.

That is not freedom.

That is chaos with rented shoes.

A lane helps you know what belongs in the show and what does not.

It helps the audience understand what they found.

It helps you plan episodes.

It helps you explain the show to guests.

It helps you sell sponsors later.

It helps you design artwork.

It helps you decide whether video matters.

It helps you know what kind of work you are signing up for.

The lane is not the prison.

The lane is the first road.

## The Big Question

Here is the question I want you to ask before choosing a format:

What is the main engine of the show?

Not the topic.

The engine.

What makes the show move?

Is it your point of view?

Is it the guest?

Is it the chemistry between hosts?

Is it the story?

Is it the research?

Is it the place?

Is it the audience interaction?

Is it the teaching?

Is it the mystery?

Is it the performance?

Is it the problem you solve?

Different engines need different formats.

If your point of view is the engine, a solo show may work.

If the guest's story is the engine, interviews may work.

If chemistry is the engine, co-hosted may work.

If suspense is the engine, documentary or audio fiction may work.

If community is the engine, local or live may work.

If expertise is the engine, teaching or business authority may work.

If the show is built around nostalgia and media memory, commentary or rewatch formats may work.

A lot of people choose format backward.

They say, "I want to do interviews" before asking whether interviews are the best engine for the idea.

Or they say, "I want a co-host" when what they really need is structure.

Or they say, "I need video" when what they really need is a clear promise.

Start with the engine.

Then pick the lane.

## Lane One: The Solo Show

The solo show is the simplest and scariest format.

It is simple because you do not need anyone else.

No guest booking.

No co-host scheduling.

No "Can you do Thursday?" emails.

No guest showing up with AirPods in a coffee shop beside an espresso machine that sounds like a jet engine.

You can record when you are ready.

You can move fast.

You can respond to current events.

You can teach.

You can tell stories.

You can build a direct relationship with the audience.

That is powerful.

It is also scary because there is nowhere to hide.

It is just you.

Your voice.

Your thoughts.

Your structure.

Your ability to keep the listener with you.

A solo show exposes whether you actually know what you want to say.

That can be uncomfortable.

But it can also be the best format for a person with a strong point of view.

## Best For

A solo show works well for:

Teachers.

Coaches.

Consultants.

Writers.

Comedians.

Commentators.

Storytellers.

Experts.

Creators with a strong personal voice.

People who want to move quickly.

People who do not want guest scheduling to control the show.

A solo show is especially good if your audience is coming to hear how you think.

Not just what you know.

How you think.

That is different.

## Hardest Part

The hardest part of a solo show is structure.

You need a plan.

If you sit down and talk for forty minutes with no shape, the listener will feel like they got trapped in a phone call with someone who keeps saying, "Anyway, long story short," and then making the story longer.

A solo show needs an outline.

Not always a script.

An outline.

The listener needs to feel movement.

Here is the problem.

Here is why it matters.

Here is the story.

Here is the lesson.

Here is the next step.

That is enough.

But you need something.

## Starter Structure

A solo episode can use this structure:

1. Hook. 2. What we are talking about. 3. Why it matters. 4. Story or example. 5. Main point one. 6. Main point two. 7. Main point three. 8. Practical takeaway. 9. Call to action. 10. Closing line.

That is not fancy.

It works.

The show can still sound natural. You can still go off-road a little. But you need to know where the road is.

## Example

Let's say the show is called **Old Dogs, New Tools**.

The promise is helping people over forty-five understand AI, media, and creative tools without feeling stupid.

A solo episode might be:

**Episode: Stop Asking AI to Be Magic**

The opening:

"Today we are talking about the mistake most beginners make with AI. They ask it one vague question, get one generic answer, and decide the tool is either useless or a miracle. It is neither. It is an assistant. And if you brief it like a lazy boss, it will work like a confused intern."

That is a solo show.

One voice.

One point.

Clear promise.

Useful example.

A little attitude.

That can work.

## Watch Out For

Do not make every solo episode a diary entry unless the show is built around diary energy.

Do not confuse vulnerability with lack of structure.

Do not assume your passion will create pacing by itself.

Do not record tired rambling and call it authenticity.

Authenticity is not an excuse to waste time.

A solo show can be raw.

It still needs to be built.

## Lane Two: The Interview Show

The interview show is probably the format most people think of first.

It makes sense.

You bring on a guest.

You ask questions.

They tell stories.

You learn things.

The guest may bring an audience.

You do not have to carry the whole episode alone.

Interview shows can be wonderful.

They can also become generic very quickly.

Because there are a lot of them.

A lot.

An interview show needs more than "I talk to interesting people."

That phrase has done enough damage.

Retire it.

Everybody thinks they talk to interesting people.

The better question is:

What kind of people, about what kind of thing, for what kind of audience, with what kind of promise?

That is the interview lane.

## Best For

An interview show works well for:

Hosts who are curious.

People with access to interesting guests.

Business builders.

Community connectors.

Local storytellers.

Industry shows.

Personal growth shows.

Creative shows.

History or legacy projects.

Shows built around lived experience.

An interview show is especially good when the guest brings stories the audience cannot get from you alone.

## Hardest Part

The hardest part is not asking questions.

The hardest part is asking questions that get past the usual answers.

Most guests have a surface-level story.

The bio story.

The website story.

The LinkedIn story.

The "I'm excited to be here" story.

Your job is to get to the human story.

What changed?

What went wrong?

What did you almost quit?

What did people misunderstand?

What did you learn the hard way?

What would you tell someone who is where you were?

That is where the show lives.

## Starter Structure

An interview episode can use this structure:

2. Cold open or strong guest moment. 2. Host welcome. 3. Why this guest matters. 4. Quick guest setup. 5. Origin question. 6. Problem or turning point. 7. Specific story. 8. Lessons learned. 9. Practical advice for listener. 10. Final question. 11. Guest links. 12. Closing.

Again, simple.

The magic is not in having a complicated structure.

The magic is in listening inside the structure.

## Example

A show called **Second Shift Stories** interviews people who started over after fifty.

A weak opening question:

"So, tell us about yourself."

That is not evil, but it is lazy.

A better opening question:

"When did you first realize the old version of your life was not going to work anymore?"

Now we are somewhere.

A follow-up:

"What did that cost you?"

Now we may have a real story.

Another follow-up:

"What did people around you not understand at the time?"

Now we may have tension.

Interview shows live in follow-ups.

The planned question starts the car.

The follow-up drives it somewhere interesting.

## Watch Out For

Do not let the guest promote for forty-five minutes.

Do not let every guest give the same advice.

Do not ask questions so long that the guest forgets what you asked.

Do not bring on guests only because they are available.

Do not confuse having a guest with having an episode.

A guest is not the show.

The conversation is the show.

## Lane Three: The Co-Hosted Show

A co-hosted show can be a blast.

When the chemistry is right, it feels alive.

Two people who know each other well can create rhythm, conflict, humor, memory, and energy that one host cannot easily create alone.

This is the garage conversation format.

The barstool format.

The diner booth format.

The sports desk format.

The two-friends-arguing-about-a-movie format.

The married-couple format.

The old-bandmates format.

The "we have been having this conversation for twenty years and finally decided to record it" format.

That can be great.

It can also go off the rails fast.

Because chemistry is not the same as structure.

A co-hosted show still needs a lane.

## Best For

Co-hosted shows work well for:

Comedy.

Sports.

Movies.

Pop culture.

Local commentary.

Reaction shows.

Advice shows.

Nostalgia.

Faith.

Politics, if you enjoy stress.

Shows built around conversation and contrast.

They work especially well when the hosts bring different strengths.

One host is the researcher.

One is the reactor.

One is the storyteller.

One is the skeptic.

One is the expert.

One is the audience stand-in.

One brings chaos.

One keeps the train somewhere near the tracks.

That balance matters.

## Hardest Part

The hardest part is not talking over each other.

The second hardest part is not turning every episode into the same conversation.

The third hardest part is scheduling, because apparently adults have lives and calendars and other nonsense.

Co-hosts need roles.

Not rigid roles.

But enough that the show does not become two people fighting for the wheel.

Who opens?

Who moves the segments?

Who reads listener questions?

Who handles sponsor reads?

Who books guests, if any?

Who edits?

Who posts?

Who makes sure the episode ends before everyone loses the will to live?

Figure it out early.

## Starter Structure

A co-hosted show can use:

3. Cold open. 2. Welcome. 3. Quick personal check-in. 4. Topic setup. 5. First take. 6. Counterpoint or story. 7. Main discussion. 8. Recurring segment. 9. Listener question or comment. 10. Takeaway. 11. Closing.

The recurring segment is your friend.

It gives the audience something familiar.

It gives the hosts a place to go.

It makes the show feel built.

## Example

A show called **Rewind Argument** features two Gen X friends revisiting movies they loved as kids to see whether they still hold up.

One host is sentimental.

The other is merciless.

That is the engine.

The show structure:

Opening clip-style question: “Did this movie age like fine wine or like a gas station hot dog?”

Segment one: What we remembered.

Segment two: What actually happened.

Segment three: The scene that still works.

Segment four: The scene that should be taken out back.

Segment five: Would we show this to our kids?

That is a co-hosted show with a lane.

Same format every week.

Different movie.

Built-in humor.

Built-in Gen X memory.

Built-in audience participation.

## Watch Out For

Do not assume your friendship is automatically entertaining.

It may be.

It may not.

Your friendship matters to you.

The audience needs a show.

Do not make every inside joke stay inside.

Bring the listener in.

If the audience feels like they are sitting at the table with you, great.

If they feel like they are listening from the hallway while you reference things they do not understand, fix it.

## Lane Four: The Documentary or Investigative Show

The documentary lane is powerful.

It is also work.

Real work.

This is not "we talk about a case for an hour after reading a Wikipedia page."

That is commentary.

Documentary means there is reporting, structure, narrative, research, interviews, archival material, pacing, and usually a reason the story needs to unfold in pieces.

This lane can be incredible for true crime, local history, business stories, sports seasons, family history, investigative reporting, or deep-dive storytelling.

But it is not the easiest starting lane.

It can be worth it.

Just do not walk into it thinking it is casual.

## Best For

Documentary shows work well for:

True crime.

History.

Investigations.

Sports seasons.

Local stories.

Business origin stories.

Community issues.

Personal journeys.

Audio journalism.

Stories with mystery, change, tension, or discovery.

They work especially well when the story has a strong question.

What happened?

Why did it happen?

Who was affected?

What changed?

What was hidden?

What did people misunderstand?

What does this story reveal about a bigger issue?

## Hardest Part

The hardest part is organizing the material.

You may have interviews, documents, timelines, locations, facts, conflicting memories, audio clips, news articles, court records, photos, music, narration, and emotional weight.

That is a lot.

A documentary show needs planning.

It needs a story map.

It needs fact-checking.

It needs ethical care.

Especially with true crime or real people.

This is not the lane where you get cute with facts.

If you are naming people, making claims, discussing crimes, talking about victims, or accusing anyone of anything, be careful.

Very careful.

## Starter Structure

A documentary episode might use:

4. Cold open scene. 2. Narrator setup. 3. What we know. 4. Main character or source. 5. Timeline movement. 6. New complication. 7. Expert or witness perspective. 8. What remains unclear. 9. Emotional or practical takeaway. 10. Next episode tease.

This is closer to storytelling than conversation.

Every piece needs to earn its place.

## Example

A local history documentary show called **Before the Bypass** tells the story of towns, businesses, and landmarks that changed when highways moved traffic away.

Episode one might open with an old diner owner describing the day the road changed.

Then the host explains the place, the timeline, and why it mattered.

Then come archival ads, local memories, city records, and a conversation with someone who worked there.

The episode is not just “remember that diner?”

It is about change.

Commerce.

Memory.

How places disappear.

What people carry with them.

That is documentary.

## Watch Out For

Do not overpromise.

Do not call something investigative if it is really a conversation.

Do not use people’s pain as decoration.

Do not stretch a two-episode story into ten because you like the sound of your own narration.

Do not ignore fact-checking.

Documentary can build trust.

It can also destroy trust quickly if handled badly.

## Lane Five: Audio Fiction

Audio fiction is one of my favorite lanes.

I am biased.

I wanted to make audio fiction from the beginning. That was one of the original creative sparks behind Rogue. We built a network, did a lot of shows, learned a lot of production, and eventually got to make *Hellhound Country*, which brought me close to that original dream.

Audio fiction is different.

It is not just talking.

It is writing.

Performance.

Sound design.

Pacing.

World-building.

Casting.

Music.

Atmosphere.

Editing.

It is a show in the old-school sense.

It can feel like radio drama, theater, film, literature, and podcasting all ran into each other in a dark hallway.

That is beautiful.

It is also not easy.

## Best For

Audio fiction works well for:

Horror.

Mystery.

Science fiction.

Comedy.

Drama.

Serialized stories.

Anthologies.

Character pieces.

Noir.

Westerns.

Weird local legends.

Anything where sound can build a world.

It is especially good when the audience likes imagination.

Audio fiction asks the listener to participate.

You give them the voices and sound.

They build the rest in their head.

That is powerful.

## Hardest Part

The hardest part is production weight.

You need scripts.

Actors or performers.

Recording quality.

Sound design.

Editing.

Continuity.

Music or sonic identity.

A release plan.

It is not impossible.

But it is heavier than two people talking.

If you are starting with audio fiction, consider a smaller format first.

A five-episode season.

A short anthology.

A narrator-driven series.

One actor.

Minimal sound design.

A story that uses limitation as style.

The Twilight Zone did not need a Marvel budget to make people uneasy.

Sometimes suggestion is stronger than spectacle.

## Starter Structure

Audio fiction can use:

5. Cold open scene. 2. Theme or title. 3. Setup. 4. Character desire or problem. 5. Strange event or complication. 6. Escalation. 7. Choice or reveal. 8. Consequence. 9. Ending button. 10. Next episode tease, if serialized.

If it is anthology, each episode needs its own complete arc.

If it is serialized, each episode needs progress and a reason to continue.

## Example

A show called **Static at Midnight** follows a late-night radio host in a desert town who starts receiving calls from people who may be dead.

That lane is clear.

Audio-first.

Fiction.

Late-night.

Creepy.

Voice-driven.

Sound matters.

The format could be:

Opening radio monologue.

Call one: strange but explainable.

Call two: personal detail the caller should not know.

Song break or station ID.

Call three: impossible.

Host tries to rationalize.

Final sound or reveal.

Sign-off that does not feel safe.

That is a show.

It has a lane.

## Watch Out For

Do not start with an enormous cast and ten locations if you have no production system.

Do not rely on sound effects to hide weak writing.

Do not make every episode confusing and call it mysterious.

Mystery creates questions.

Confusion creates frustration.

Know the difference.

## Lane Six: The Local or Community Show

Local shows are underrated.

Everybody talks about reaching the world, and that is great.

But reaching a town can matter.

A neighborhood.

A school district.

A sports community.

A local business scene.

A music scene.

A church community.

A regional culture.

A city full of stories that nobody is recording.

Local shows can build real trust because the audience has shared context.

They know the streets.

They know the teams.

They know the restaurants.

They know the old businesses.

They know the weather.

They know the arguments.

They know the weird intersection nobody designed correctly.

That gives you texture.

## Best For

Local shows work well for:

Local history.

High school sports.

Business spotlights.

Community leaders.

Restaurants.

Events.

Local politics.

Arts and music.

Forgotten places.

Regional identity.

They are especially good for creators who already have relationships in the community.

## Hardest Part

The hardest part is avoiding small-town Facebook energy.

You know what I mean.

Drama.

Rumors.

Passive-aggressive comments.

People wanting free promotion.

Businesses wanting coverage but not wanting to sponsor.

Everybody knowing everybody.

Local can be powerful, but it requires boundaries.

What is the show?

What do you cover?

What do you not cover?

How do people submit stories?

What does sponsorship cost?

What is editorial and what is advertising?

Be clear.

## Starter Structure

A local show might use:

6. Local hook. 2. Main story or guest. 3. Place/context. 4. Why it matters now. 5. Memory/history. 6. Community voice. 7. Upcoming events or ways to connect. 8. Sponsor or partner mention. 9. Closing.

This format can be audio, video, or both.

Video may help if place matters.

Audio may help if conversation and memory matter.

## Example

A show called **Gone But Not Forgotten Waco** tells stories about closed restaurants, old businesses, local hangouts, and places that shaped people's memories.

That show could be fun because it has nostalgia, local pride, community input, and sponsor potential.

Episode:

"The Elite Cafe: More Than a Sign"

The host talks about the place.

A guest tells a memory.

A listener sends in a story.

You talk about what businesses like that meant before everything became more standardized.

A local sponsor fits naturally.

That is a local show with a lane.

## Watch Out For

Do not become free advertising for everyone.

Do not let the loudest commenters decide the show.

Do not cover everything.

Local does not mean random.

A local show still needs a promise.

## Lane Seven: The Business or Authority Show

A business show does not have to be boring.

It often is.

But it does not have to be.

A business or authority show is built to create trust around expertise.

It may not make money directly from ads.

It may make money by leading to clients, consulting, speaking, workshops, books, courses, services, sponsorships, or partnerships.

This is important.

Not every show is monetized the same way.

If a show brings you one good client, that may matter more than thousands of downloads.

### Best For

Business shows work well for:

Consultants.

Coaches.

Agencies.

Attorneys.

Financial professionals.

Real estate professionals.

Medical or wellness experts, with care.

Tech educators.

Small business owners.

Authors.

Speakers.

People who need trust before sales.

They work best when the show teaches, explains, demonstrates judgment, and builds relationship.

## Hardest Part

The hardest part is not turning the show into a sales pitch.

Nobody wants to listen to a forty-minute brochure.

The show should help the audience.

If you help enough, the business benefit follows.

That does not mean hiding what you sell.

It means earning trust before asking for money.

## Starter Structure

A business show can use:

7. Problem the audience has. 2. Why it matters. 3. Common mistake. 4. Story or client-style example. 5. Framework or solution. 6. What to do next. 7. Soft call to action.

This format can be very effective.

It is also good for SEO because each episode can answer a real question people search.

## Example

A show called **The Plain-English AI Office** helps small business owners understand how AI can save time without making their business sound fake.

Episode:

“Five Tasks AI Can Take Off Your Plate This Week”

The host explains each task, gives examples, warns what not to automate, and offers a downloadable checklist.

That show may lead to consulting.

The show is useful first.

The business comes after trust.

## Watch Out For

Do not speak in jargon.

Do not make every episode an ad.

Do not pretend to know more than you know.

Do not give legal, medical, or financial advice casually if your field is high-stakes.

Be useful.

Be careful.

Be human.

## Lane Eight: The Teaching or How-To Show

A teaching show is built around helping people learn something.

It can be solo, interview, video, audio, or hybrid.

The engine is usefulness.

This is a good lane if you like explaining things.

And if people have told you, "You make this make sense," pay attention.

That is a gift.

Teaching shows can cover almost anything:

Podcasting.

AI.

Gardening.

Cooking.

Fitness.

Woodworking.

Career change.

Parenting.

Writing.

Local history research.

Music.

Technology.

Faith.

Money.

The key is to teach in a way the audience can actually use.

## Best For

Teaching shows work well for:

Educators.

Coaches.

Experts.

Hobbyists.

Technical people who can speak human.

People who like frameworks.

People with patience.

People who enjoy breaking things down.

## Hardest Part

The hardest part is not overwhelming the listener.

When you know a lot, you may want to tell everything.

Do not.

One episode should not be a junk drawer of knowledge.

Teach one useful thing.

Then the next one.

Then the next.

Bird by bird.

Lesson by lesson.

## Starter Structure

A teaching episode can use:

8. What you will learn. 2. Why it matters. 3. The common mistake. 4. Step one. 5. Step two. 6. Step three. 7. Example. 8. Quick recap. 9. Homework or next step.

Simple.

Useful.

Repeatable.

## Example

A show called **Start Simple Studio** teaches older creators how to make their first show.

Episode:

"How to Record a Test Episode Nobody Hears"

The host explains why testing matters, how to set it up, what to listen for, and what not to worry about yet.

That is useful.

That is a lane.

## Watch Out For

Do not turn every episode into a lecture.

Use stories.

Use examples.

Use mistakes.

Use humor.

People learn better when they feel like a person is teaching them, not a textbook with a microphone.

## Lane Nine: The Nostalgia or Media Commentary Show

This lane is tempting for Gen X because we have a lot of media memory.

Movies.

TV.

Music.

Commercials.

Games.

Toys.

Sports moments.

Video stores.

Radio.

Magazines.

Mall culture.

Saturday morning cartoons.

The Sears Christmas catalog, which was basically Amazon made of paper and hope.

Nostalgia can be powerful.

But nostalgia alone is not enough.

A good nostalgia show is not just "remember this?"

It needs an angle.

What does it mean now?

Does it hold up?

What did we learn from it?

What did it get wrong?

How did it shape us?

Why does it still matter?

Why did we think this was normal?

That last question can carry a whole series.

## Best For

Nostalgia/media shows work well for:

Movies.

Music.

TV.

Sports history.

Pop culture.

Generational reflection.

Comedy.

Rewatch shows.

Parent/child comparisons.

Cultural commentary.

## Hardest Part

The hardest part is avoiding listicle energy.

"Top 10 Things Only 80s Kids Remember" has its place, but it can get thin fast.

The better show uses nostalgia as a doorway into story, identity, humor, and meaning.

### Starter Structure

A nostalgia episode can use:

9. Memory hook. 2. What we thought then. 3. What it looks like now. 4. What still works. 5. What aged badly. 6. What it says about us. 7. Listener memory prompt. 8. Closing.

### Example

A show called **Still Holds Up?** revisits movies, songs, toys, shows, and cultural moments from Gen X childhood.

Episode:

"Did The Breakfast Club Help Us Understand Teenagers, or Did It Just Give Us Better Soundtrack Taste?"

That is a lane.

It is funny.

It is reflective.

It gives the audience a reason to listen beyond memory.

### Watch Out For

Do not make nostalgia a museum.

Make it a conversation.

The past is more useful when it helps us understand the present.

## Lane Ten: The Hybrid Show

A hybrid show combines formats.

Maybe it is mostly solo, with occasional interviews.

Maybe it is a co-hosted show with documentary segments.

Maybe it is an audio show with video clips.

Maybe it is a local show with teaching episodes.

Maybe it is a business show with personal stories.

Hybrid shows can be great.

But they are dangerous at the beginning.

Because hybrid can become a polite word for unfocused.

Before you go hybrid, know the primary lane.

Primary lane first.

Extras second.

## Best For

Hybrid shows work well when the main promise is clear but the format needs flexibility.

For example:

A creator show may have solo teaching episodes, guest interviews, and occasional case studies.

A local history show may mix interviews, field recordings, and narration.

A business show may include solo lessons and client-style stories.

A horror show may include fiction episodes and behind-the-scenes creator notes.

That can work.

Because the promise holds it together.

## Hardest Part

The hardest part is keeping the audience oriented.

If episode one is a solo rant, episode two is a two-hour interview, episode three is a fiction piece, episode four is a live panel, and episode five is a cooking video, people may wonder what on earth they subscribed to.

That does not mean you cannot experiment.

It means you need to label things.

Use seasons.

Use segments.

Use episode titles.

Use a clear show description.

Tell the audience what is happening.

Do not make them guess.

## Starter Structure

A hybrid show can use categories:

Main episodes.

Interviews.

Short lessons.

Field notes.

Bonus episodes.

Listener questions.

Behind-the-scenes.

Name the categories.

That helps.

## Example

This book could become a hybrid show.

Main episodes teach a chapter concept.

Interview episodes feature creators over forty-five.

Short clips answer common questions.

Bonus episodes review tools.

Listener episodes answer real questions.

The promise holds it together:

Helping people who remember the old media world create real shows with new tools.

That is the lane.

The formats support it.

## Watch Out For

Do not use hybrid as an excuse to avoid choosing.

Choose the promise.

Choose the primary engine.

Then let the format flex around it.

## Picking the Lane: A Simple Scorecard

Here is a practical way to choose.

For each format, rate it from one to five.

How excited am I to make this?

How easy is it to produce?

How well does it serve the audience?

How much does it fit my strengths?

How much does it fit my schedule?

How much does it fit my budget?

How likely am I to still be doing this after ten episodes?

That last one matters most.

A format that scores high on excitement but low on sustainability may be a season two idea.

A format that scores high on sustainability but low on excitement may become boring.

You need both.

Not perfect.

Balanced.

## Your Strengths Matter

Pick a format that uses what you already do well.

If you are naturally curious, interview.

If you are opinionated and clear, solo.

If you are funny with a friend, co-host.

If you love research and story, documentary.

If you love writing and atmosphere, audio fiction.

If you know everyone in town, local.

If you teach well, how-to.

If your work builds trust, business authority.

If your memory is full of old media, nostalgia commentary.

Do not ignore your strengths because someone online said the "best format" is something else.

The best format for them may be wrong for you.

You are not building their show.

## Your Weaknesses Matter Too

Be honest about what drains you.

If scheduling guests makes you want to throw your calendar into a river, do not build a guest-heavy show unless you have help.

If editing video makes you miserable, do not start with a complicated video show.

If talking alone scares you so much you never record, maybe start with a co-host or interviews.

If research overwhelms you, do not start with investigative documentary.

If writing scripts feels impossible, maybe audio fiction should wait or start smaller.

This is not quitting.

This is design.

A good lane uses your strengths and respects your limits.

## The First-Ten-Episodes Rule

Whatever lane you choose, commit to it for ten episodes.

Ten is long enough to learn.

Ten is short enough not to feel like a life sentence.

During those ten episodes, do not keep changing everything.

Do not change the title every week.

Do not switch from solo to interview to documentary to cooking show because the numbers were weird.

Do not add video on episode three because someone on LinkedIn said video is the future.

Do not panic.

Make the first ten.

Then review.

Ask:

Did this format fit me?

Did it serve the audience?

What part felt strong?

What part dragged?

Could I keep doing this?

What should change for the next ten?

That is how the show grows.

## A Lane Can Become a Road

A starting lane is not the whole journey.

It is the beginning.

A solo show can add interviews.

An interview show can add solo commentary.

A co-hosted show can become live.

A local show can add video.

A business show can become a course.

An audio fiction show can become a live reading.

A nostalgia show can become a community.

A teaching show can become a book.

A show can become more than you imagined.

But it needs a first shape.

Pick the lane.

Make the first version.

Learn from it.

Then widen the road.

## Closing Thought

A show idea can stay dreamy forever if you never pick a lane.

That may feel safe.

It is not.

It is just another way to not start.

Pick the lane that fits the promise, the audience, the engine, and your actual life.

Solo.

Interview.

Co-hosted.

Documentary.

Fiction.

Local.

Business.

Teaching.

Nostalgia.

Hybrid.

There is no perfect answer.

There is only the best starting answer.

Choose it.

Commit to the first ten.

Let the show teach you what it wants to become.

And remember:

The lane is not the prison.

It is the road that lets you finally move.

# Chapter 5: Tell the Story So People Stay

## Memory, conflict, scenes, stakes, humor, and why details beat summaries.

A show can have the right microphone, a decent name, clear artwork, good lighting, a real website, clean show notes, a smart AI workflow, and a sponsor deck that looks like somebody grown made it.

And still be boring.

That is the part nobody wants to hear.

Because we like to think the tools will save us.

They will not.

Tools help.

Structure helps.

Good audio helps.

Video helps.

Clips help.

Search helps.

AI helps.

But the thing that makes people stay is usually older than all of that.

Story.

Not story in the fancy literary sense where everybody has to stare out a window while rain represents regret.

I mean story in the human sense.

Something happened.

Somebody wanted something.

Something got in the way.

Somebody changed.

Somebody learned.

Somebody lost.

Somebody found.

Somebody made a mistake.

Somebody survived.

Somebody finally said the thing out loud.

That is story.

And story is why people stay.

Information can get someone to click.

Story gets them to keep listening.

Advice can be useful.

Story makes the advice stick.

Facts can be important.

Story gives facts a place to live.

A good story is not decoration.

It is delivery.

It is how human beings have been carrying meaning around since before anybody thought it was a good idea to put a microphone on a desk and call it a content strategy.

So if you are making a show, you need to learn how to tell the story.

Not perfectly.

Not like some novelist in a cabin.

Like a person who knows when something matters and can help somebody else feel why.

## A Story Is Not "Something Happened"

Let's start here.

A story is not just something that happened.

That is an event.

A story is what changed because something happened.

This matters because people often tell stories like they are giving a report.

"I went to the store. I saw this guy. He said something funny. Then I came home."

That may be true.

It is not necessarily a story yet.

What changed?

Why does it matter?

What was at stake?

What did you expect?

What surprised you?

What did it reveal?

What did you learn?

What did it make you feel?

A story needs movement.

The movement can be big.

A person loses a business and starts over.

A family secret comes out.

A coach changes a kid's life.

A town loses a landmark.

A creator finally launches the show after years of talking about it.

But the movement can also be small.

You thought one thing, then realized another.

You expected a guest to be funny, and they became emotional.

You went looking for a simple answer and found a bigger question.

You remembered something from childhood and realized it shaped how you see the world now.

That is enough.

The change is the story.

If nothing changes, the listener may wonder why they are there.

And they are allowed to wonder.

Their time is not free.

## Summary Is the Enemy of Feeling

Most people summarize when they should tell a scene.

They say:

"My grandfather was a hard worker."

Okay.

That tells me something.

But it does not make me feel anything yet.

Now tell me this:

"My grandfather got up every morning at 4:30. Not 4:35. Not when he felt like it. 4:30. The coffee pot made that little burnt smell old coffee pots used to make, and by the time the rest of the house moved, he had already been outside long enough for his boots to be wet."

Now I know him.

I can see him.

I can smell the coffee.

I can hear the house.

I can feel the discipline.

That is the difference.

Summary gives information.

Scenes create memory.

And a show needs memory.

If you want people to remember the episode, give them something to see, hear, feel, or repeat.

Do not only tell us the conclusion.

Take us to the moment.

## The Scene Test

Here is a simple test.

When you are telling a story, ask:

Where are we?

Who is there?

What time of day is it?

What does it look like?

What does it sound like?

What did you want?

What went wrong?

What did someone say?

What changed?

You do not need every detail.

Too many details can become a hostage situation.

But the right details make the scene real.

Let's say you are telling a story about starting your show.

Weak version:

"I was nervous before recording the first episode."

Better version:

"I sat there for twenty minutes looking at the red record button like it had personally wronged me. The mic was ready. The outline was sitting there. Nobody else was in the room. And somehow that was worse, because now there was nobody to blame if I sounded stupid."

That is a scene.

Same information.

More feeling.

The listener has been there.

Maybe not with a microphone, but with something.

A first job interview.

A hard phone call.

A blank page.

A test.

A doctor's appointment.

A conversation they did not want to have.

Specific details make the story more universal, not less.

That sounds backwards, but it is true.

The more specific the moment, the more likely someone recognizes the feeling.

## Details Beat Big Words

A lot of people try to make a story powerful by using big emotional words.

It was devastating.

It was amazing.

It was terrifying.

It was life-changing.

It was hilarious.

Those words may be true.

But they are labels.

They tell the listener what to feel instead of giving them the evidence.

Do not just say it was devastating.

Show me the empty office.

Show me the keys on the desk.

Show me the email.

Show me the phone call.

Show me the person sitting in the car afterward because they were not ready to go inside yet.

Do not just say it was hilarious.

Tell me what happened.

Tell me who said what.

Tell me why everybody lost it.

Tell me the one detail that still makes you laugh ten years later.

Do not just say it was scary.

Tell me what the room sounded like.

Tell me what you thought was going to happen.

Tell me what your body did.

Details carry emotion better than labels.

The audience does not need you to announce the feeling.

They need you to create the conditions for the feeling to arrive.

## Before and After

A simple story structure is before and after.

Before, I thought this.

After, I understood this.

Before, I was afraid to start.

After, I realized the first version did not have to be perfect.

Before, I thought podcasting was about microphones.

After, I realized it was about the promise.

Before, I thought my story was ordinary.

After, I realized ordinary stories get powerful when you pay attention.

Before, I thought AI would make things fake.

After, I learned it could carry some of the weight if I kept my voice in it.

This structure works because it creates movement.

It does not have to be dramatic.

It just has to show a shift.

A lot of good teaching uses before and after.

A lot of good comedy uses before and after.

A lot of good interviews use before and after.

A lot of good memoir uses before and after.

In a show, before and after gives the listener a reason to stay.

They want to know how the change happened.

## Want, Obstacle, Change

Here is another simple structure.

Somebody wanted something.

Something got in the way.

Something changed.

That is story.

A host wanted to start a show.

Fear got in the way.

They recorded a test episode anyway and learned the fear was survivable.

A local business owner wanted to keep the restaurant open.

The highway moved traffic away.

The town changed, and the restaurant became a memory.

A guest wanted to reinvent themselves after fifty.

Age, money, and doubt got in the way.

They built something smaller first and found momentum.

A parent wanted to record family stories.

Awkwardness and procrastination got in the way.

Then a health scare made the recording urgent.

Want.

Obstacle.

Change.

You can build almost any story with those three pieces.

If a story feels flat, check which piece is missing.

No want?

The listener does not know what anyone cares about.

No obstacle?

There is no tension.

No change?

There is no reason it mattered.

## Conflict Does Not Always Mean Fighting

When people hear the word conflict, they think arguing.

That is one kind.

But conflict can be quieter.

Conflict can be uncertainty.

A choice.

A risk.

A deadline.

A misunderstanding.

A secret.

A fear.

A gap between what someone wants and what is possible.

A person trying to change but not knowing how.

A host trying to ask a hard question without losing the guest.

A family trying to talk about the past without reopening every wound.

A business trying to stay alive.

A creator trying to publish before they feel ready.

That is conflict.

It does not need screaming.

In fact, some of the best conflict is internal.

"I wanted to start, but I was afraid I would look stupid."

That is a real conflict.

A lot of your audience will understand that one immediately.

Especially if they are the kind of people this book is for.

They have lived long enough to know most battles do not come with theme music.

They come with hesitation, bills, pride, fear, old habits, family obligations, and a calendar that looks like somebody lost a bet.

Conflict is whatever makes the outcome uncertain.

Use that.

## Stakes: Why Does It Matter?

Stakes are what make the story matter.

What happens if this fails?

What happens if the person does not change?

What happens if the story is never told?

What happens if the show does not get made?

The stakes do not have to be life and death.

Sometimes the stakes are emotional.

"If I never make this show, I think I will always wonder if I could have."

That is a stake.

Sometimes the stakes are relational.

"If I do not record my father's stories now, I may lose them."

That is a stake.

Sometimes the stakes are business.

“If I cannot explain what I do, people will keep choosing the louder competitor.”

That is a stake.

Sometimes the stakes are creative.

“If I keep waiting until I am ready, I will never make anything.”

That is a stake.

Do not assume the audience knows why it matters.

Tell them.

But do not overdo it.

You do not need dramatic music under everything like a reality show about competitive cake decorating.

Just make the importance clear.

## The Gen X Story Advantage

I think Gen X, and people around that age, have a strange story advantage.

We remember a lot of transitions.

We remember before and after.

Before the internet and after.

Before smartphones and after.

Before streaming and after.

Before everybody carried a camera and after.

Before social media and after.

Before AI and whatever this is turning into now.

That gives us natural story structure.

We have lived through change.

And stories are about change.

We remember when music videos felt revolutionary.

We remember when cable felt endless because it had thirty-six channels and that seemed like outer space.

We remember when calling someone meant calling their house and possibly talking to their parent first, which was a whole social obstacle course.

We remember when you had to wait for photos to be developed and sometimes found out two weeks later that half of them were your thumb.

We remember when a show came on at a certain time, and if you missed it, you missed it.

We remember the old ways.

But we also use the new tools.

That is not just nostalgia.

That is material.

A show can use that.

Your stories can connect past and present.

They can say:

Here is how this used to work.

Here is how it works now.

Here is what got better.

Here is what got worse.

Here is what we lost.

Here is what we gained.

Here is what still matters.

That is a rich lane.

Do not waste it by only saying, "Remember this?"

Ask what it means.

## Nostalgia Is a Doorway, Not the Whole House

Nostalgia is powerful.

It is also cheap if you use it badly.

"Remember Saturday morning cartoons?"

Yes.

Now what?

"Remember Blockbuster?"

Yes.

Now what?

"Remember MTV?"

Yes.

Now what?

A good show uses nostalgia as a doorway into something deeper.

Why did Saturday morning cartoons matter?

Because they were ritual.

Because they gave kids a shared world.

Because they were appointment television.

Because the toy commercials were basically tiny sales attacks on our developing brains.

Because they taught us structure, characters, theme songs, cliffhangers, and identity.

Why did video stores matter?

Because choice became physical.

Because browsing was part of the experience.

Because cover art mattered.

Because staff recommendations mattered.

Because the shelf told you what category something belonged to.

That connects directly to show packaging now.

Why did MTV matter?

Because it taught us that sound and image together could create identity fast.

That connects to short-form clips now.

Nostalgia becomes useful when it helps explain the present.

Otherwise, it becomes a museum tour with better music.

## Humor Helps People Stay

Humor matters.

Not every show needs to be a comedy show.

But humor helps people breathe.

It lowers defenses.

It makes hard truths easier to hear.

It makes the host feel human.

It gives the audience something to repeat.

It creates rhythm.

It can make practical advice less dry.

A little humor can turn a lesson from "homework" into "I can keep listening."

That matters for this audience.

Most of us have sat through enough boring meetings, training videos, school assemblies, church announcements, mandatory HR modules, and conference breakout sessions where the PowerPoint had seventy-eight bullet points and no mercy.

We do not need more of that.

If you can make the point with a little life in it, do it.

But do not force jokes.

The best humor usually comes from truth.

The drawer full of cables.

The fear of the record button.

The mic arm that cost more than your first car payment.

The AI answer that sounds like a motivational speaker trapped in a spreadsheet.

The way every project somehow turns into needing one more password.

That is real.

That is funny because it is recognizable.

Humor should serve the story.

Not hijack it.

## The Specific Is What People Remember

People remember specifics.

Not “my childhood was different.”

They remember:

The TV with the dial.

The smell of the video store carpet.

The sound of the cassette clicking.

The blue screen when the VCR had no tape.

The Pizza Hut red cups.

The school projector cart.

The teacher rolling in the TV and everyone realizing the day had just improved by 400 percent.

The first time you heard your voice on an answering machine and thought, “No, absolutely not.”

Those details do work.

They do not just create nostalgia.

They create trust.

They tell the audience:

This person was there.

This person remembers.

This person notices.

That is why details matter in any kind of story.

If you are telling a business story, give us the office, the email, the meeting, the number on the invoice.

If you are telling a family story, give us the kitchen, the chair, the smell, the phrase someone always said.

If you are telling a sports story, give us the field, the weather, the scoreboard, the kid who did not look like much until the fourth quarter.

If you are telling a creator story, give us the mic, the room, the fear, the first comment.

Specifics make stories feel true.

And true-feeling stories keep people listening.

## Do Not Start Too Far Back

This is a common storytelling problem.

Someone wants to tell a story about why they started a show, and they begin with:

"Well, I was born in..."

No.

Unless the hospital was haunted or the doctor handed you a microphone, we probably do not need to start there.

Start closer to the moment something changed.

You can go back later if needed.

But do not make the listener sit through the entire family tree before the story begins.

A good question is:

Where does the trouble start?

Or:

Where does the choice start?

Or:

Where does the surprise start?

Start there.

If you need background, add it after the listener cares.

This is how movies often work.

They do not always explain everything first.

They drop you into a moment.

Then you learn what you need as you go.

Shows can do that too.

Start where the energy is.

## Do Not Explain the Lesson Too Early

Another mistake is telling the lesson before the story.

"I learned that you should never give up."

Okay.

Now the story has less tension because you told me the bumper sticker version first.

Let the listener experience the story.

Then pull out the lesson.

If you say:

"I was sitting in the parking lot outside the studio, trying to decide whether to go in. I had already told three people I was starting this show. I had the mic. I had the notes. I had no excuse left except fear."

Now I want to know what happened.

Then later you can say:

"That was the first time I realized getting started is not a feeling. It is a decision you make while fear is still in the room."

That lesson lands harder because the story carried it.

Do not rob your own story by explaining it too soon.

## The Story Spine

Here is a useful story spine for shows:

Once, things were like this.

Then something happened.

Because of that, this changed.

But there was a problem.

So someone had to make a choice.

That choice led to this.

And now things are different.

That works for a lot of stories.

Example:

Once, podcasting felt like something only tech people did.

Then smartphones made listening easy.

Because of that, regular people started building listening habits.

But the creator side still felt intimidating.

So people had to choose whether to learn the tools or stay out.

That choice led to a new wave of creators.

And now AI is changing the process again.

That is a story.

It has movement.

It has cause and effect.

Try using that spine when an episode feels like a pile of thoughts.

A pile of thoughts is not a story.

A story has movement.

## The Interview Story

If you are interviewing someone, your job is to help them tell a story, not just answer questions.

A lot of guests will speak in summaries.

They are used to bios, resumes, sales pitches, LinkedIn profiles, and short answers.

You have to invite them into scenes.

Instead of:

“What was that like?”

Try:

“Where were you when you realized it was not working?”

Instead of:

“Tell me about your business.”

Try:

"What was the first day like when it was real and not just an idea?"

Instead of:

"What advice would you give?"

Try:

"What mistake taught you that?"

Instead of:

"How did you feel?"

Try:

"What did you do right after the call ended?"

Those questions pull people into moments.

Moments create stories.

Stories create connection.

## The Follow-Up Is Where the Story Is

The first answer is often not the story.

It is the headline.

The follow-up is where the story starts.

Guest:

"It was a hard season."

Host:

"What made it hard?"

Guest:

"We were broke and the business was struggling."

Host:

"Was there a specific moment when you realized it was worse than you thought?"

Guest:

"Yeah. I remember sitting in the parking lot outside the bank..."

There it is.

The parking lot.

Now we are in a scene.

If you had moved on after "hard season," you would have missed the story.

Listen for the door.

Then open it.

## The Host Can Tell Stories Too

Even if you have guests, your stories matter.

The host's stories create trust.

They tell the audience why you are the one guiding the conversation.

That does not mean you make every guest's story about you.

We all know that person.

Guest: "I survived a terrible thing."

Host: "That reminds me of the time my sandwich order was wrong."

No.

Do not do that.

But a short host story can set context, build connection, and make the guest feel safer.

The trick is to use your story as a bridge, not a roadblock.

A host story should usually be short.

It should serve the episode.

It should point back to the guest or the listener.

It should not become a hostile takeover.

## Story, Then Lesson, Then Use

For practical shows, a good pattern is:

Story.

Lesson.

Use.

Tell the story.

Pull out what it means.

Show the listener how to use it.

Example:

Story:

"I spent three weeks comparing microphones instead of recording because buying gear felt safer than hearing my own voice."

Lesson:

"Gear can become procrastination with a receipt."

Use:

"Before you buy anything else, record a two-minute test with what you already have."

That works.

It gives the audience emotion, meaning, and action.

A lot of practical shows only give lesson and use.

That can be helpful, but it may not be memorable.

The story makes it stick.

## Do Not Tell Every Story You Know

This may be hard for some of us.

Just because you have a story does not mean it belongs in this episode.

A story should serve the promise.

If the episode is about choosing a show format, do not spend ten minutes telling a story about your uncle's boat unless the boat somehow explains the format.

Maybe it does.

Families are strange.

But be honest.

Does the story help?

Does it reveal something?

Does it move the episode?

Does it make the point clearer?

Does it create connection?

If not, save it.

A good story in the wrong place becomes a detour.

And too many detours make the listener wonder whether you know where you are going.

Keep a story bank.

Write down stories as they occur to you.

Use them when they belong.

Not just because you remembered them.

## The Story Bank

Every creator should keep a story bank.

This can be a notebook, a document, a notes app, a spreadsheet, voice memos, index cards, whatever works.

Capture stories under categories:

Childhood.

Work.

Family.

Failure.

Starting over.

Technology.

Creative fear.

Funny moments.

Lessons learned.

Guests.

Local memories.

Objects.

Places.

Media that shaped you.

Mistakes.

Turning points.

Then tag them by use:

Good for opening.

Good for teaching.

Good for humor.

Good for sponsor story.

Good for AI chapter.

Good for voice chapter.

Good for launch chapter.

Good for audience chapter.

This may sound too organized for something as messy as memory.

But you will forget things.

You will be in the middle of an episode and think, "I had a perfect story for this," and it will vanish like your car keys five minutes after you were holding them.

Capture the stories.

Future you needs the help.

## Storytelling for Business Shows

Business shows need story more than people think.

A lot of business content is painfully dry.

Frameworks.

Tips.

Strategies.

Best practices.

Thought leadership.

Words that sound useful until everyone says them and they turn into beige wallpaper.

Story fixes that.

Instead of:

"Consistency is important for brand growth."

Say:

"I worked with a client who changed their offer every two weeks. Every time the audience started to understand what they did, they changed the sign on the door. They thought they were improving. They were actually erasing the trail."

That is a story.

Now the lesson makes sense.

Business stories do not have to reveal private client information.

You can anonymize.

You can create composite examples.

You can tell your own mistakes.

You can describe patterns.

Just make the idea live somewhere.

## Storytelling for Local Shows

Local shows are built on story.

Not just information.

The city council agenda matters to some people.

But the story is:

Who is affected?

What changed?

Why does this place matter?

What did it used to be?

Who remembers?

What is being lost?

What is being built?

What does this say about the town?

A local business closing is not only a fact.

It is where people had first dates, birthday dinners, awkward job interviews, after-game meals, and Sunday lunches.

A school is not only a building.

It is hallways, teachers, football games, cafeteria smells, lockers, band concerts, friendships, and people still telling stories about something that happened in 1989.

Local storytelling works when it understands that places hold memory.

Bring the memory out.

## Storytelling for Audio Fiction

Audio fiction is all story.

But even there, the basics matter.

Want.

Obstacle.

Change.

Scene.

Stakes.

Specific details.

Sound.

Audio fiction has a special advantage: sound can suggest more than it shows.

A phone ringing in an empty room.

A screen door.

A distant train.

A storm.

A chair moving upstairs when nobody is supposed to be there.

A voice on a radio that says the host's name before the host introduced himself.

Sound creates story space.

But sound does not replace story.

Atmosphere is not plot.

A creepy vibe is not enough.

Something has to happen.

Someone has to want something.

Something has to change.

Otherwise, it is just fog with a microphone.

## Storytelling for Teaching Shows

Teaching shows need examples.

Examples are little stories.

If you are explaining SEO, show the difference between an episode called "Episode 12" and an episode called "Why New Creators Quit After Episode Six."

If you are explaining AI prompts, show the bad prompt and the better prompt.

If you are explaining sponsor readiness, tell the story of the host who tried to sell before they had three episodes.

If you are explaining voice fear, take us to the moment someone listens back for the first time.

Teaching without examples can feel abstract.

Examples make it usable.

Stories make it memorable.

## The Ending Button

A story needs an ending button.

Not always a big dramatic ending.

Just a line, image, realization, or moment that tells the listener, "That is why this mattered."

It might be funny.

It might be emotional.

It might be practical.

It might be quiet.

Example:

"And that was the day I realized I had spent three weeks shopping for microphones because buying something was easier than becoming someone who records."

That is an ending button.

Or:

"He never did reopen the diner. But every time someone talks about that corner, they still call it by the restaurant's name. That is how you know a place mattered."

That is an ending button.

Or:

"The first episode was not good. But it existed. And once it existed, I had something to fix."

That is an ending button.

Do not just let stories fade out.

Land them.

## Let the Audience Finish Some of It

You do not have to explain every feeling.

Sometimes the strongest thing you can do is trust the audience.

Give them the scene.

Give them the line.

Give them the action.

Then let them feel it.

This is hard because hosts like to explain.

We want to make sure the listener got it.

But overexplaining can weaken a story.

If the story already shows the lesson, do not beat the listener with the lesson until it stops moving.

Say enough.

Then let it breathe.

A good audience is smarter than your insecurity thinks they are.

## The Story Checklist

Before using a story in an episode, ask:

What is the point of this story?

Where does it start?

What changed?

Who wanted something?

What got in the way?

What are the stakes?

What specific detail makes it feel real?

What line or moment should the audience remember?

Does this story serve the episode promise?

Where does it end?

If you cannot answer those, the story may need more work.

Or it may not belong in this episode.

That is okay.

Save it.

The right story in the right place is powerful.

The wrong story in the wrong place is just a scenic route to nowhere.

## Practice: Turn a Summary Into a Scene

Here is a practice exercise.

Take a summary:

"I was nervous before launching my show."

Now turn it into a scene.

Where were you?

What time was it?

What were you looking at?

What did your body feel like?

What did you almost do instead?

What finally made you press publish?

Now write that.

It may become:

"I had the episode uploaded and ready to go, and I still sat there for ten minutes with the cursor over the publish button. The house was quiet. The dog was asleep. Nobody knew I was about to do it, which made it feel both safer and worse. I kept thinking, once I click this, I am not a person thinking about making a show anymore. I am a person who made one. That scared me more than I expected."

That is a scene.

The same idea became something someone can feel.

Do this often.

It will change the show.

## Closing Thought

Story is not the fancy part.

Story is the human part.

It is how people understand change.

It is how advice becomes memorable.

It is how facts become meaningful.

It is how a host becomes familiar.

It is how a guest becomes more than a bio.

It is how a listener decides to stay.

You do not have to be a novelist.

You do not have to make every episode dramatic.

You do not have to turn your show into a therapy session with theme music.

You just need to notice the story inside the thing you are saying.

What changed?

What mattered?

Where were we?

Who wanted what?

What got in the way?

What did it cost?

What did we learn?

Tell that.

Tell it clearly.

Tell it with enough detail that we can see it.

Tell it with enough honesty that we believe you.

Tell it with enough structure that we can follow.

That is how you keep people.

Not tricks.

Not gimmicks.

Not louder thumbnails.

Story.

The oldest tool in the room.

Still undefeated.

# Chapter 6: Don't Build a Studio Before You Build a Habit

There is a moment that happens to a lot of new creators. They finally get excited. They have the idea. They have maybe even written down a few episode topics. They can picture themselves doing it. Maybe they have already told a friend, "I think I'm going to start a show."

Then they go online.

That is where the trouble starts.

All of a sudden they are looking at microphones, cameras, mixers, lighting kits, boom arms, sound panels, headphones, editing software, hosting platforms, AI tools, studio desks, backdrops, and people on YouTube explaining why their $1,800 setup is actually "pretty basic." And just like that, the excitement turns into panic.

The first question is not, "What is the best setup?" The first question is, "What is enough for me to start?" Enough to record clearly. Enough to hear yourself and your guest. Enough to publish without being embarrassed. Enough to learn. Enough to make the next episode.

Do not build a studio before you build a habit.

## The Gear Trap

Buying equipment feels like progress. I get it. I love gear. I love production. I love a room that looks and sounds right. But gear can become procrastination with a receipt. It lets you feel like you are working while avoiding the vulnerable part: recording something and hearing yourself try.

You probably need less gear than you think. And if your show is unclear, better gear will not save it. A great microphone will not make a boring show interesting. A beautiful camera will not give you a point of view. A mixer will not create chemistry. The gear should support the show. It should not become the show.

## What You Actually Need

For most beginners, the starter setup is simple: a microphone, wired headphones, a quiet-enough place to record, a computer or phone, recording software, a way to edit, a host or publishing platform when ready, and a plan for the episode.

That is it. Not a soundproof studio. Not a $700 microphone. Not a mixer with colorful buttons. Not a camera that makes you look like you are filming a Netflix documentary.

Start with a simple dynamic USB microphone if you can. Dynamic mics are forgiving in normal rooms, and USB keeps things simple. Use wired headphones. Wireless earbuds are great for walking around Target pretending you do not need more storage bins, but recording is different. Wired headphones reduce delay and help keep audio clean.

The room matters. Rugs help. Curtains help. Couches help. Bookshelves help. Clothes in a closet help. You do not have to soundproof your room at the beginning. You just need to make it less echoey and less annoying.

Mic technique is free. Stay close to the mic. Keep your distance consistent. Do not lean back, turn away, check your phone, and then wonder why you sound like you are recording from another county.

## Video Can Wait, Unless It Should Not

Video adds work. Camera. Lights. Framing. Background. Storage. Thumbnails. Clips. Captions. The whole circus.

Does video make the show better? Not "is video popular?" It is. Not "does YouTube matter?" It does. But does video make your show better enough to justify the work?

If yes, start simple: a phone or webcam, decent light, clean background, and good audio first. If no, start audio-first. A good audio show that continues is better than a video show that dies after two episodes because the process was too heavy.

## When to Rent a Studio

There is nothing wrong with renting a studio. If technology stresses you out, rent the room. If you want better sound and video right away, rent the room. If you need accountability, rent the room. If you want to walk in, record, and let someone else handle the technical pain, rent the room.

That is not failure. That is using a system.

But do not rent a studio because you think you are not real without one. A clear kitchen-table show can beat a confused studio show all day.

## The Upgrade Rule

Upgrade when the show earns the upgrade. That might mean money, but it might also mean consistency. If you have made ten episodes and you know you are going to keep going, maybe upgrade the mic. If video is clearly helping after twenty-five episodes, upgrade the lighting. If editing is killing you, pay for help or improve the workflow.

Upgrade to remove friction. Do not upgrade to feel legitimate.

## The Minimum Viable Studio

Let's define the minimum viable studio.

Not the dream studio.

Not the "someday when we have sponsors and a neon sign" studio.

The smallest setup that lets you record something listenable and repeatable.

For one person, that might be:

A USB dynamic microphone.

Wired headphones.

A laptop.

A quiet room with a rug and curtains.

A simple recording app.

A folder where the files go.

That is a studio.

Not a fancy one.

Not one that makes people take photos for Instagram.

But if it lets you make the show, it counts.

For two people in the same room, you may need two microphones, two sets of headphones, and either a mixer/interface or a recording setup that can handle both inputs.

For remote guests, you need a reliable recording platform, a guest checklist, and a backup plan.

That is enough to begin.

The danger is that people think a studio has to look like a studio.

It does not.

A studio is a system for capturing the show.

That can be a spare bedroom.

That can be an office.

That can be a rented room.

That can be a corner of a closet if you are comfortable in there.

The only thing it cannot be is so complicated that you avoid using it.

## The Test Episode Nobody Hears

Before you launch, record a test episode that nobody hears.

I mean nobody.

Not the public.

Not your high school friend who tells you everything is awesome.

Not your aunt who still thinks Facebook comments are private.

Nobody.

Record the test for learning.

This is where you find out if the room echoes.

This is where you find out if the microphone is too far away.

This is where you find out if your chair squeaks like a haunted gate.

This is where you find out if the dog barks every time the mail truck comes by.

This is where you find out if your co-host's internet sounds like it is being powered by a potato.

This is also where you learn how long it takes to set up, record, save, and edit.

That matters.

A lot of people underestimate the total time.

They think, “The episode is thirty minutes, so I need thirty minutes.”

No.

You need setup time.

Recording time.

Mistake time.

File-saving time.

Editing time.

Exporting time.

Upload time.

Show notes time.

Promotion time.

The test episode tells you what the real process looks like.

That is valuable.

It is better to discover the process is too heavy before you promise the audience a weekly show.

## Remote Recording Is Not a Shortcut Unless You Prepare

Remote recording is wonderful.

It lets you interview people anywhere.

It saves travel.

It opens up guests who would never come to your studio.

It makes your show bigger than your zip code.

But remote recording is not magic.

Guests do not automatically know how to sound good.

Some will record from a kitchen.

Some will use laptop speakers.

Some will not wear headphones.

Some will have a ceiling fan chopping the air above them like a helicopter that got lost.

Some will take the call from a coffee shop because apparently chaos is part of their brand.

That is why guest prep matters.

Before the recording, send simple instructions.

Wear headphones.

Choose a quiet room.

Use a microphone if you have one.

Close other apps.

Turn off notifications.

Plug in the laptop.

Avoid Wi-Fi dead zones.

Put pets somewhere else if possible.

Join a few minutes early.

This is not being picky.

This is protecting the listener.

Bad guest audio makes the audience work harder.

Most people will not work that hard for a show they just found.

## Backup Everything

I know backups are boring.

So is insurance.

So are smoke detectors.

So is having a spare tire until you need one.

Backup your recordings.

Have a plan.

Save the raw files.

Export the finished file.

Keep a copy somewhere other than the computer you recorded on.

Use cloud storage, an external drive, or both.

Name your files clearly.

Do not have a folder full of things called:

final_mix.wav

final_final_mix.wav

actual_final_mix.wav

use_this_one_maybe.wav

episode7_NEW_REAL_FINAL_2.wav

That way lies madness.

Use a simple system.

ShowName_Ep001_Raw_Date

ShowName_Ep001_Edit_Date

ShowName_Ep001_Final_Date

Boring?

Yes.

Useful?

Also yes.

Future you will thank current you.

Future you is already dealing with enough.

## File Organization Is Part of Production

Your show needs a folder system.

Again, not glamorous.

But necessary.

A simple folder might look like this:

Show Name

- 00_Admin
- 01_Episode_Assets
- 02_Raw_Recordings
- 03_Edits
- 04_Final_Exports
- 05_Artwork
- 06_Show_Notes
- 07_Clips
- 08_Sponsor_Assets
- 09_Archive

You can make it simpler.

You can make it more detailed later.

But have something.

If you are making a show every week, the files will multiply like rabbits with Wi-Fi.

Get organized before the mess becomes a second job.

## The Room Checklist

Before recording, do the room check.

Is the fan off?

Is the AC about to kick on?

Is the refrigerator humming?

Is there traffic noise?

Is the phone silenced?

Are notifications off?

Is the mic selected?

Are the headphones plugged in?

Are the levels good?

Is the guest ready?

Is the camera framed if using video?

Is the chair quiet?

Is the dog about to become a co-host?

This takes two minutes.

It can save the whole episode.

Do not skip it because you feel awkward.

Awkward is cheaper than rerecording.

## Renting vs. Owning

Some people should buy gear.

Some people should rent a studio.

Some people should do both.

The decision is not about pride.

It is about friction.

If owning the gear makes the show easier, own it.

If owning the gear turns you into a part-time IT department, rent.

If you need guests in person and want the show to feel polished, rent.

If you are testing an idea and need to keep cost low, start at home.

If your show is sponsor-facing and professional presentation matters early, get help.

There is no one right answer.

The wrong answer is letting the setup become the reason nothing happens.

## The Real Upgrade Is Confidence

At first, gear feels like the upgrade.

Later, you learn that confidence is the upgrade.

Knowing how to use the mic.

Knowing how to fix a small problem.

Knowing how to get a guest comfortable.

Knowing how to start recording without turning it into a ceremony.

Knowing how to save the file.

Knowing how to publish.

Knowing how to recover when something goes wrong.

That confidence comes from reps.

Not purchases.

You get it by recording.

You get it by making mistakes.

You get it by solving the same problem three times until it stops being scary.

That is why the habit matters more than the studio.

The habit makes you capable.

The studio only makes you equipped.

## Closing Thought

You do not need to look like a professional creator before you become one. You become one by making episodes.

The setup should help you make the next episode. If the gear makes you excited, great. If the gear makes you freeze, simplify it. There is no one correct setup. There is only the setup that lets you keep going.

# Chapter 7: Audio, Video, or Both?

There was a time when this question was easier. A podcast was audio. You put on headphones, got in the car, walked the dog, cleaned the kitchen, or sat in the driveway for seven extra minutes because the story had not landed yet.

That still matters. Audio is not dead. Audio is intimate. A voice in your ear feels different than a face on a screen. It becomes part of someone's routine. A good audio show can feel like companionship.

But the world changed. People watch shows now. Sometimes they watch the full episode. Sometimes they watch clips. Sometimes they discover the show on YouTube, Spotify, Facebook, Instagram, or TikTok and then listen later. Sometimes they never become audio listeners at all. They think of podcasts as something to watch.

That does not mean every show needs video. It means every creator needs to make the decision on purpose.

## When Audio Makes Sense

Audio-only may be the right choice if you are brand new, if your show is story-driven, if your topic does not need visuals, if you are doing audio fiction, essays, personal stories, teaching, or intimate conversations, or if video makes you so nervous you will never start.

A consistent audio show is better than a video show that disappears because the lights, camera, background, clips, and thumbnails became a second job with no paycheck.

Do not let video kill the show before the show has a chance to live.

## When Video Helps

Video can help people connect with the host. It can show facial expressions, reactions, chemistry, guest energy, props, demonstrations, locations, charts, and the vibe of the room. Sports, comedy, business interviews, pop culture, reactions, education, and personality-driven shows often benefit from video.

Video also gives you more to work with. A full episode can become clips. Clips can become Shorts, Reels, TikToks, LinkedIn posts, Facebook posts, sponsor samples, and guest promo material. Video can be the front porch. Audio can still be the living room.

But video adds work. Not a little work. Work.

You have to know your actual life. If you have a full-time job, family responsibilities, health issues, limited energy, and no editing help, video may not be the best starting point. Not because video is bad. Because the show needs to survive.

## Doing Both

Doing both can be powerful if you have a system. Record once, publish the audio, publish the video, create clips, write show notes, post to the website, send the guest a share kit. That sounds great. It also sounds easier than it is.

"Put it everywhere" is not a plan. A plan says: we record on Tuesday, publish audio Thursday, publish video Thursday, make three clips, post one to YouTube Shorts, one to Facebook/Instagram, one to LinkedIn if it fits, and put the transcript on the website.

That may still be too much. But at least it is real.

## Short-Form Is a Doorway

Short-form clips are not the show. They are doorways into the show.

A good clip has to stand on its own. It teaches something, makes someone laugh, creates tension, gives an opinion, shows a reaction, asks a good question, or reveals a piece of the story. The worst clips feel like you walked into the middle of a conversation and nobody tells you why you should care.

Do not make clips just to make clips. Make clips because the episode created moments worth sharing. AI can help find the moment, but the moment still has to exist.

## The Old World and the New Tools

People who remember the old media world have an advantage here. We remember radio, records, tapes, CDs, VHS, cable, MTV, video stores, appointment television, newspapers, magazines, and actually having to wait for things. We also watched streaming, YouTube, smartphones, social media, podcasting, short-form video, and AI show up.

We understand audio. We understand visual storytelling. We understand long-form. We also understand the world moved whether we liked it or not. That gives us a bridge. We can use the patience and storytelling instincts of the old world with the tools of the new one.

Not to become younger. Not to pretend we were born online. To use these tools like grown people with stories.

## The Decision

Choose audio-only if you need the simplest sustainable path. Choose video if the visual connection makes the show better or helps discovery enough to justify the work. Choose both if you have the system, time, and support. Choose short-form as a discovery layer, not a substitute for a clear show.

And if you are not sure, start audio-first and test video. You do not have to publish everything you record. That is a freeing thought.

## The Audio-First Test

If you are not sure where to begin, try the audio-first test.

For the first ten episodes, make the show as clean audio.

No complicated video setup.

No full studio buildout.

No thumbnails that take three hours each.

Just record clear audio, publish consistently, and see whether the show has a pulse.

During those ten episodes, pay attention.

Are people listening?

Are they responding?

Do you enjoy the format?

Can you keep making it?

Are there moments that would have worked better on video?

Are guests asking about video?

Are listeners asking where they can watch?

Are clips harder because you have no visuals?

If the answer is yes, video may be worth adding.

If the answer is no, audio may be doing its job.

This is not about fear.

It is about evidence.

Audio-first is not anti-video.

It is a way to keep the show alive long enough to make a smarter video decision.

## The Video-First Test

Some shows should start with video.

If the host's personality is highly visual, video may help.

If the show includes demonstrations, reactions, body language, visual examples, products, maps, art, food, sports clips, local places, or live interaction, video may be part of the core experience.

For video-first shows, the test is not "Can we make it look perfect?"

The test is:

Can we make it watchable enough and repeatable enough?

That means:

Clear audio.

Good enough lighting.

A stable camera.

A clean or intentional background.

A simple thumbnail style.

A basic edit.

A publishing system.

Do not let video become a Hollywood production unless the show actually needs that.

A lot of watchable shows work because the conversation, personality, and topic are strong.

The camera just lets people feel closer to it.

## The "Record Both, Publish One" Strategy

There is a middle path.

Record both audio and video, but only publish one at first.

This can be useful if you are testing video without committing to the full video workflow.

Set up one camera.

Record the conversation.

Publish the audio.

Then watch the video privately.

Ask:

Do we look comfortable?

Does video add anything?

Are there good clips?

Is the background distracting?

Would the audience benefit from watching?

Can we handle the extra editing?

After a few episodes, you will know more.

This strategy also lets you get used to being on camera without immediately making that fear public.

That can be a gift.

Especially if you are in the "why does my face do that when I think?" phase.

We all have one.

## Short-Form Without Losing the Show

Short-form can help discovery, but it can also warp the show if you are not careful.

Some creators start making the long episode only as raw material for clips. That can work for some shows, but it can also make the full show feel hollow.

The clip should serve the show.

The show should not become a slave to the clip.

If you build every conversation around "what will make a thirty-second moment," you may miss the deeper thing.

The good news is that strong long-form episodes naturally create strong clips.

A sharp opinion.

A story with a turn.

A guest revealing something honest.

A useful explanation.

A funny exchange.

A hard truth.

Those moments clip well because they were real moments first.

So do not chase clips by making the show shallow.

Make the show better.

Then clip the best parts.

## Platform Behavior Matters

People behave differently on different platforms.

On podcast apps, people often commit to longer listening.

On YouTube, packaging and the first minute matter a lot.

On Facebook, local and familiar faces may travel better than slick branding.

On LinkedIn, practical business lessons may work better than personal rambling.

On Instagram and TikTok, short moments need to make sense quickly.

On email, the audience has already given you more trust than a random social viewer.

That means the same episode may need different packaging in different places.

The full audio title may be clear and practical.

The YouTube title may need to be more curiosity-driven.

The short clip may need a sentence that sets up the moment.

The email may need a personal note from the host.

This sounds like a lot because it can be.

That is why you do not need to start everywhere.

Pick the main platform for the full show.

Pick one or two discovery channels.

Build the habit.

Then expand.

## The Gen X Advantage in Format

People who grew up around older media forms often understand pacing better than they realize.

We watched shows that took time.

We listened to albums in order.

We waited through commercials.

We watched music videos as little movies.

We sat through news magazines, late-night interviews, sports pregame shows, sitcoms, dramas, and cable oddities.

That gave us a feel for format.

Openings mattered.

Theme music mattered.

Segments mattered.

Commercial breaks mattered.

Endings mattered.

Even weird shows had structure.

That matters now.

A modern creator can combine that old-school understanding of shape with modern distribution.

A show can have a clear open like television, intimacy like radio, discoverability like YouTube, clips like social media, and workflow help from AI.

That is not nostalgia.

That is using everything available.

## When to Add Video Later

Add video when it solves a real problem or creates real opportunity.

Add video when:

The audience asks for it.

The host is comfortable enough to be watchable.

The guest format benefits from visual connection.

Clips are clearly part of the growth strategy.

Sponsors would value video visibility.

YouTube discovery fits the audience.

The production system can handle it.

Do not add video because you feel guilty.

Guilt is not a media strategy.

Do not add video because a stranger online said podcasts are dead.

They are not.

Do not add video because you want to feel more legitimate.

A bad video workflow will make you feel less legitimate very quickly.

Add it when it helps.

## The First Season Format Contract

Whatever you choose, make a first-season contract with yourself.

For the first ten episodes, I will make the show this way.

That is it.

Not forever.

Ten episodes.

This gives you enough time to learn without constantly changing the format because you got nervous.

If you change everything every week, you will never know what worked.

Make a plan.

Test it.

Review it.

Then decide.

## Closing Thought

Audio is not dead. Video is not magic. Short-form is not a strategy by itself.

The best format serves the listener, fits the show, and survives your real life.

# Chapter 8: Name the Show So People Know What They Found

Naming things is hard. You can know the audience, the format, the first ten episodes, and exactly why you are doing it. Then someone asks, "What's it called?" and your brain turns into a junk drawer.

Your show name has a job. Its job is not to prove how clever you are. Its job is not to sound like a mysterious indie band from 1997. Its job is to help the right person understand what they found.

## Don't Be Too Cute

I like clever. I like wordplay. I like weird references. But there is a difference between clever and confusing. Clever opens the door. Confusing hides the door and blames the listener for not bringing a flashlight.

A lot of creators pick names that mean something to them personally but nothing to anyone else. An inside joke. A phrase from childhood. Something vague and moody. Something that looks good on a T-shirt but does not tell anyone what the show is.

That can work if you already have an audience. Most of us do not have that luxury. Most of us need the name to do some work.

If your show is about starting over after fifty, old horror movies, local sports, grief, classic country, AI tools, small-town history, or audio fiction set in West Texas, the name should give me a clue.

Do not make people solve a puzzle before they know whether they care.

## The Grocery Store Test

Imagine your show is sitting on a shelf. Somebody is walking by. They are busy, tired, and surrounded by other choices. Does the name tell them enough to stop?

Not whether it makes sense after a five-minute explanation. Not whether your best friend likes it. Does a stranger get it fast enough to care?

A title can be clever if the subtitle does the explaining. "Second Shift" could be anything. "Second Shift: Stories of Starting Over After 50" tells me where I am.

The title can have personality. The subtitle can do the work.

## Say It Out Loud

Say the name out loud. Then imagine introducing it at dinner. Imagine a guest saying, "I was on a show called..." Imagine someone hearing it in a noisy room and trying to search for it later.

Does it work? Is it easy to spell? Is it too close to something else? Does it need punctuation no one will remember? Does it depend on a clever spelling that will make people hate you when they try to find it?

Easy is not lazy. Easy is kind.

## Check What Already Exists

Search podcast apps, YouTube, Google, and social platforms. Check the domain. Check trademarks if you are building a serious brand.

A good name should not start its life in a traffic jam.

## Give It Room to Grow

Do not name the show too narrowly if you already know it wants room. "My First 30 Days With AI" might be a short series. "Learning AI After 50" has more room. "The Second Half Creator" has even more.

Can the name survive fifty episodes? Can it survive guests, video, live events, sponsors, or the show getting better?

## Bad Names Can Still Teach You

When you brainstorm names, let the bad ones come out.

Do not judge too early.

The first round of names may be terrible.

That is fine.

Sometimes the terrible names are just clearing the pipes.

Write them down anyway.

The too-obvious ones.

The too-cute ones.

The ones that sound like a 1994 alternative band.

The ones that sound like a consulting firm.

The ones that sound like a true crime show even though you are talking about gardening.

The ones that make you laugh but would make no sense to anyone else.

Get them out.

Then look for what they are trying to say.

Maybe three bad names all point to the same emotion.

Maybe the title is wrong but the subtitle is good.

Maybe the word you keep using is the real clue.

Maybe the name is not there yet, but the category is clearer.

Brainstorming is not picking.

It is digging.

## Genre Cues Matter

A show name gives genre signals.

People can often feel what kind of show something is before they fully understand it.

A name can sound like:

A comedy.

A local show.

A business show.

A true crime show.

A horror fiction series.

A sports show.

A faith show.

A self-help show.

A history show.

A nostalgia show.

A tech show.

That can help or hurt.

If you call a serious business show "The Dumpster Fire Hour," that may be funny, but it sends a message.

Maybe the message is right.

Maybe it is not.

If you call a funny Gen X nostalgia show "The Intergenerational Media Memory Project," I am already asleep.

The name needs to fit the emotional promise.

Ask:

What genre does this name sound like?

Does that match the actual show?

Would the right listener feel invited?

Would the wrong listener be confused in a useful way?

That last one is not bad.

A name can repel the wrong people a little.

That is allowed.

## Name Examples: Weak, Better, Stronger

Let's play with examples.

Weak:

**The Mike Show**

Unless Mike is already famous, this does not tell us enough.

Better:

**Mike Talks Media**

Clearer, but still broad.

Stronger:

**Dial-Up Wisdom: Making Shows in the Age of AI**

Now we know the world, the audience, and the angle.

Weak:

**Unfiltered Conversations**

This could be anything. Also, everyone is apparently unfiltered now, which usually means the filter needed to be cleaned, not removed.

Better:

**Second Act Conversations**

Better, but still broad.

Stronger:

**Second Act Stories: People Starting Over After 50**

Now there is a person and a promise.

Weak:

**The Haunted Mic**

Could be fun, but what is it?

Better:

**The Haunted Mic: Audio Fiction and Late-Night Horror**

Now we know the genre.

Stronger:

**The Haunted Mic: Original Horror Stories for the Late-Night Crowd**

That is clearer and still has mood.

The point is not to copy these.

The point is to see how clarity and personality can work together.

## The Subtitle Is Your Safety Net

If you have a title you love but it is not clear enough, do not throw it away immediately.

Try adding a subtitle.

Title:

**Static at Midnight**

Could be a music show, a horror show, a radio show, or a show about insomnia.

Subtitle:

**Static at Midnight: Strange Stories From the Edge of the Dial**

Now it has a world.

Title:

**The Long Way Around**

Could be travel, grief, business, recovery, or road trips.

Subtitle:

**The Long Way Around: Starting Over, One Story at a Time**

Now it points somewhere.

Title:

**Old Dogs, New Tools**

Probably a show about older people learning technology. Good. Clear. Funny enough.

Subtitle:

**AI, Media, and Creativity for People Who Remember Dial-Up**

Now it has personality.

Use the subtitle to make the promise clear.

The title can carry feeling.

The subtitle can carry explanation.

## Ask the Right People

Do not ask everyone if they like the name.

Ask the kind of person who might actually listen.

And do not ask, "Do you like it?"

Ask better questions.

What do you think this show is about?

Who do you think it is for?

What kind of tone do you expect?

Would you remember it?

Could you spell it?

Does it sound like something else?

Would you click it if the topic mattered to you?

This is useful feedback.

“Do you like it?” is dangerous because people may answer based on personal taste, not clarity.

Your brother-in-law may hate the name.

That does not matter unless he is the audience.

Your friend may love the name because they love you.

That is nice and not very useful.

Ask for understanding, not approval.

## Using AI for Names

AI can help brainstorm names.

It can also give you names that sound like startup companies selling anxiety as a service.

Use it carefully.

Give AI the show promise, audience, tone, and examples of names you like and hate.

Ask for:

Clear names.

Funny names.

Serious names.

Names with subtitles.

Names that are less cute.

Names that are more searchable.

Names that sound like a real show, not an app.

Then do not accept the first batch.

Push.

Ask for plainer.

Ask for warmer.

Ask for more Gen X without making it a nostalgia museum.

Ask for names that avoid clichés.

AI is good for options.

You still need taste.

You still need to say the name out loud.

You still need to check availability.

You still need to decide.

## Legal and Brand Caution

I am not your lawyer.

That is probably good for everyone.

But I will say this: if you plan to build a serious brand, check the name.

Do a basic search.

Look through podcast apps.

Look through YouTube.

Search trademarks if the show is part of a business.

Check domain names.

Check social handles.

Look for confusingly similar names.

If another show has the same name and topic, do not talk yourself into using it anyway.

You are not being bold.

You are creating a future mess.

Pick something else.

A show name should help you start clean.

Not start with a confusing argument.

## Closing Thought

A great name will not make a bad show good. But a bad name can make a good show harder to find. Clarity is an advantage. Memorability is an advantage. Searchability is an advantage.

Be creative. Be interesting. Be yourself. Just do not be confusing.

# Chapter 9: Make It Look Like the Show It Is

Now that we have talked about naming the show, we need to talk about what it looks like.

This is where a lot of people panic. "I am not artistic." Fair. Not everybody knows fonts, color theory, or why one design looks professional and another one looks like a garage sale flyer where the printer was losing hope.

Good news: your artwork does not have to be a museum piece. It has to be clear.

Cover art is not decoration. It is a signal. It tells people, "This is the kind of show this is." Funny. Serious. Local. Mysterious. Smart. Warm. Weird. Professional. Nostalgic. Practical.

## Design for Small

Most people are not seeing your artwork as a giant poster. They are seeing it as a little square on a phone next to twenty other little squares. If your art only works when it is big, it does not work.

Tiny text is a problem. Too many words are a problem. Low contrast is a problem. Busy backgrounds are a problem. Five faces, two microphones, a skyline, three logos, a sponsor badge, and a picture of your dog may all mean something to you, but at thumbnail size it becomes visual soup.

And nobody orders visual soup.

Shrink it down. Look at it on your phone. Put it next to other shows. Ask someone else what they see. If they cannot read it, it is not done.

## Do Not Default to Microphones

Please be careful with microphones, headphones, sound waves, and generic podcast icons. A microphone tells me it is a podcast, but I already know that. The microphone is not the promise. The subject is the promise.

If your show is about old horror movies, show me that world. If it is about local sports, show me that energy. If it is about starting over after fifty, show me that feeling. If it is about AI for regular people, show me the bridge between human and tool.

Using a microphone for every show is like putting a picture of a fork on every restaurant sign. Yes, we know eating is involved. But what kind of place is it?

## DIY, Designer, or AI?

You can make your own art with Canva, Adobe Express, templates, stock photos, simple typography, or AI image tools. Keep it simple: one strong idea, one or two fonts, big readable text, strong contrast, breathing room.

You can also hire a designer. That may be smart if the show is serious, business-related, sponsor-facing, or something you plan to build around. But a designer cannot decide what the show is for you. Give them the audience, tone, examples, colors, and what not to do.

AI can help brainstorm visuals and mood boards. It can also make things look like a robot's dream about a podcast. Watch for weird details, unreadable words, glossy nonsense, and hands that appear to have been assembled during a power outage.

AI can help create art. It cannot replace taste.

## Face or No Face?

If the show is built around you, your reputation, personality, or relationship with the audience, your face may help. If nobody knows who you are yet, your face alone may not be enough. A face plus a clear title can work. A face plus a vague title may not.

For fiction, documentary, mystery, history, or concept-driven shows, the show may need a symbol, place, mood, or object instead.

## YouTube Thumbnails Are Different

Podcast cover art is the identity of the show. A YouTube thumbnail sells one episode or moment. Thumbnails may need larger faces, fewer words, stronger contrast, clearer emotion, and a reason to click.

But do not make every thumbnail look like the host just saw a raccoon steal a wallet. Dignity is still allowed.

## Build a Small Visual System

Artwork is not only the cover.

Eventually, the show may need:

Podcast cover art.

YouTube thumbnails.

Social quote cards.

Guest announcement graphics.

Clip covers.

Newsletter headers.

Sponsor one-sheets.

Website banners.

Live event posters.

Merch, if the world gets weird in your favor.

That does not mean you need all of it on day one.

Please do not build a full brand system before recording a test episode unless you are being paid by the hour.

But it does mean your cover art should point toward a larger visual world.

Pick a few basics:

Two or three colors.

One main font.

One secondary font.

A thumbnail style.

A photo or illustration style.

A rule for guest graphics.

A rule for episode titles.

A basic layout.

This is not about making everything sterile.

It is about making things recognizable.

Recognition builds trust.

If someone sees your clip in a feed, they should eventually know it is yours before reading the logo.

That is what a visual system does.

## Typography Is Not Just Decoration

Fonts have personalities.

Some fonts feel serious.

Some feel playful.

Some feel old.

Some feel modern.

Some feel cheap.

Some feel like they belong on a haunted carnival poster.

Some should be taken behind the shed and gently retired.

Choose fonts that match the show.

A practical AI-for-older-creators show probably needs clear, readable type. Maybe a little retro flavor, but not so much that it looks like a parody of 1986.

A horror fiction show can get moodier.

A local history show can use texture and place.

A sports show can be bold.

A business show can be clean.

But whatever you choose, readability wins.

If the title cannot be read at thumbnail size, the font failed.

It may be beautiful.

It may be interesting.

It may have cost money.

It still failed.

## Color Sends a Message

Color does a lot of work.

Bright colors can feel energetic, funny, young, loud, or playful.

Dark colors can feel serious, cinematic, mysterious, premium, or heavy.

Muted colors can feel thoughtful, nostalgic, calm, or mature.

High contrast can help visibility.

Low contrast can look elegant at full size and invisible on a phone.

Again, context matters.

The color palette should match the promise.

If your show is comforting and practical, a harsh neon palette may feel wrong.

If your show is loud, funny, and sports-driven, soft beige may not carry enough energy.

If your show is horror fiction, pastels probably need a very good reason.

Do not pick colors only because you like them.

Pick them because they help the show tell the truth.

## The Face Problem

If your face is on the cover, use a good photo.

Not necessarily an expensive photo.

A good photo.

Clear.

Well-lit.

Sharp.

Not a selfie from below your chin where you look like you are checking whether the phone still has service in a basement.

If you are building a personality-driven show, the photo should communicate who you are on the show.

Warm.

Funny.

Serious.

Direct.

Curious.

Trustworthy.

Strange in a good way.

Whatever fits.

If you are using multiple hosts, do not cram everyone into a tiny square unless their faces are part of the promise.

For some shows, host photos are perfect.

For others, they are unnecessary.

Do not make your face carry a concept it cannot explain.

A face plus a vague title is still vague.

## Episode Art vs. Show Art

Your main show art is the overall identity.

Episode art is optional, but it can be useful.

Some shows use the same cover every time.

That is fine.

Some shows use guest photos or episode-specific art.

That can help with sharing, especially on YouTube, social media, and websites.

But episode art adds work.

If you are already overwhelmed, do not add a custom art burden to every episode.

Start with the main cover.

Then create a simple reusable template for episode graphics.

Guest name.

Episode title.

One strong photo or visual.

Show logo.

Readable layout.

That is enough.

Do not make each episode look like a different show.

Consistency matters.

## Thumbnails Are Tiny Billboards

A YouTube thumbnail is not the same as cover art.

It is a tiny billboard for one episode.

It needs to sell the specific click.

But do not confuse selling the click with lying.

A thumbnail should create interest.

It should not promise something the episode does not deliver.

If the episode is calm and useful, do not make the thumbnail look like a building exploded.

If the episode is a serious conversation, do not put a fake shocked face on it unless something genuinely shocking happens.

If your audience is grown adults, respect them.

They can handle a thumbnail that does not scream.

A good thumbnail is clear, specific, readable, and emotionally accurate.

## Design Review Questions

Before approving artwork, ask:

Can I read it at phone size?

Does it match the title?

Does it match the tone?

Does it look like the audience it is for?

Does it stand out without lying?

Does it look intentional?

Would I be proud to put this on a sponsor sheet?

Would a guest be proud to share it?

Does it still work in black and white?

Does it look dated in a bad way or timeless in a good way?

Does it feel like the show?

That last one matters most.

A cover can be technically good and still wrong.

Listen to that.

## When to Redesign

Do not redesign every time you get insecure.

That is just Resistance with a color palette.

But do redesign when the art no longer matches the show.

Maybe the show grew up.

Maybe the first cover was too amateur.

Maybe the format changed.

Maybe the audience changed.

Maybe the title stayed but the promise got clearer.

Maybe the visual quality is hurting credibility.

That is fine.

Redesign thoughtfully.

Do not surprise the audience with a completely different identity unless you are intentionally relaunching.

A redesign should clarify the show.

Not erase its memory.

## Closing Thought

The cover is not where every idea goes. It is where the main idea goes.

Make it honest. Make it readable. Make it fit. Make it look like the show it is.

# Chapter 10: Where Does the Show Live?

At some point, after the idea, name, artwork, format, and recording plan, you run into another question: where does this thing go?

This is where the word podcast comes roaring back into the room whether I like it or not. We are making a show. But when it comes time to distribute it, we deal with hosting platforms, RSS feeds, podcast apps, video platforms, analytics, players, embeds, and monetization tools.

We do not worship the technical stuff. We understand it enough to make good decisions.

## The Simple Version

A show usually needs four things: a place to store the files, a way to distribute the show, a place where the audience can find episodes and information, and a way for you to stay connected to the audience.

For audio, a podcast host stores your audio file and creates an RSS feed. The RSS feed is the pipe that sends the show to apps like Apple Podcasts, Spotify, and others. Most listeners never think about RSS. Good. They should not have to. You just need to respect the pipe.

For video, things can be different. YouTube is a platform. Spotify supports video. Some creators upload full video separately from audio. There are several ways to do it.

The important question is: where will the audience find the show, and where do you want them to go next?

## Hosting Is Infrastructure

A hosting platform does not make your show good. It stores it, publishes it, distributes it, gives analytics, may provide a basic website, and may offer monetization or social tools.

That is infrastructure. The host gets the show out there. You still have to make something worth coming back to.

Free hosting can make sense when testing an idea. But free often has tradeoffs: limited analytics, basic websites, limited storage, limited support, branding restrictions, or moving pains later. Paid hosting is not automatically better either. Do not pay for features that only make you feel legitimate.

Pay for what solves a real problem.

## Your Show Needs a Home Base

Not necessarily on day one. But eventually, yes, probably.

A home base gives people one clear place to understand what the show is. It can hold the description, host bio, episodes, contact info, guest form, sponsor page, newsletter signup, transcripts, links, and anything else that helps people go deeper.

Your website is also where search engines and AI tools can better understand your show. An audio file sitting inside an app is not always easy for the wider internet to understand. A clear episode page with title, summary, transcript, links, and guest information gives the show a trail.

If a sponsor asks, "What is this show?" send them to a page. If a guest asks, "What do you need from me?" send them to a page. If a listener wants to contact you, they should be able to find the form without needing a map and emotional support.

## Platforms Are Rented Land

YouTube is rented land. Facebook is rented land. Instagram, TikTok, X, LinkedIn, Spotify, Apple — all platforms you do not control.

Use them. Use the heck out of them if they help. But do not confuse access with ownership.

A platform can change rules, algorithms, layouts, visibility, account access, or what worked yesterday. If your whole audience relationship lives inside those platforms, you are vulnerable.

That is why the boring stuff matters. Website. Email list. Clear links. Contact forms. Backups.

Nobody brags at dinner about a clean contact form. But boring infrastructure can save you later.

## Email Still Matters

Email sounds old. Good. Old things sometimes work.

An email list gives you a direct connection to people who asked to hear from you. You do not need a complicated newsletter at first. Send new episodes, a short note from the host, behind-the-scenes thoughts, links from the show, a monthly recap, or the best starting episodes.

Do not spam people. If someone gives you permission to show up in their inbox, treat that like a privilege.

## The Basic Home Base

A simple show website should include a homepage, listen/watch buttons, episode pages, about/host page, contact page, guest inquiry page if needed, sponsor page if needed, newsletter signup, and links to major platforms.

That is enough. You do not need thirty pages. You need a clear path.

## Link Hubs Are Not Homes

A link hub can be useful.

A page with all your links is better than making people search through five apps and three social profiles like they are on a scavenger hunt at a mall in 1992.

But a link hub is not the same as a home base.

A link hub points.

A home base explains.

A link hub says, "Here are the doors."

A home base says, "Here is what this is, who it is for, where to start, how to connect, and why you might care."

At the beginning, a link hub may be enough as a temporary bridge.

But do not confuse temporary with permanent.

If the show matters, build a place that belongs to the show.

A simple one-page website can do more for clarity than a beautifully chaotic social profile.

## The Start Here Page

One of the most useful pages a show can have is a Start Here page.

This is especially true after you have more than ten episodes.

New listeners do not want homework.

They do not want to scroll through every episode and guess which one explains the whole thing.

Give them a door.

Your Start Here page might include:

A short welcome.

What the show is.

Who it is for.

Three to five best first episodes.

A short note about the host.

The main subscribe/follow buttons.

A newsletter signup.

A contact link.

That is enough.

This page is helpful for listeners, guests, sponsors, and even you.

When someone asks, "Where should I begin?" you have an answer.

Do not make new people dig through the attic before they find the front door.

## Sponsor and Guest Pages Are Not Just Extras

If you plan to have guests, build a guest page.

If you plan to sell sponsorships, build a sponsor page.

These pages do not need to be fancy.

They need to reduce friction.

The guest page answers:

What is the show?

Who listens?

How long does recording take?

Is it audio, video, or both?

What setup do I need?

What should I prepare?

What links or bio should I send?

The sponsor page answers:

What is the show?

Who does it reach?

What is the audience like?

What sponsorship options exist?

How do I contact someone?

When these pages exist, you look more professional.

More importantly, you save time.

You stop writing the same email over and over like you are trapped in a customer-service time loop.

## Owning the Relationship

Your website and email list matter because they help you own the relationship.

You do not own your Facebook followers.

You do not own your YouTube subscribers.

You do not own your Instagram reach.

You are allowed to talk to those people when the platform decides to let you.

That does not make platforms bad.

It makes them platforms.

Email is different.

A person gives you permission to contact them directly.

That is valuable.

Treat it carefully.

Do not spam people.

Do not send empty announcements.

Do not email only when you want something.

Send something worth opening.

A note.

A recap.

A link.

A question.

A story behind the episode.

A useful resource.

A first-look at the next show.

The email list is not old-fashioned.

It is durable.

And durable things are underrated until everything else breaks.

## Choosing a Host Without Losing Your Mind

When choosing a podcast host, do not start by comparing every feature from every company.

Start with what you need.

Do you need audio-only?

Video support?

Good analytics?

A simple website?

Easy distribution?

Dynamic ads?

Team access?

Transcripts?

Private feeds?

Monetization tools?

Low cost?

Reliable support?

Migration options?

A beginner does not need everything.

Pick the host that makes publishing easier and does not trap you.

Ask:

Can I afford this for a year?

Can I understand it?

Can I move my RSS feed later?

Does it distribute where my audience listens?

Does it give me enough data to learn?

Will it make me dread publishing?

If the answer to that last one is yes, keep looking.

The tool should reduce friction.

Not become a second show.

## Closing Thought

Your show can live on many platforms, but it should not be homeless.

Platforms are where people may find you. Your home base is where they understand you.

# Chapter 11: Don't Hide Your Show From the Internet

A lot of creators think uploading the episode is the finish line.

It is not.

Uploading means the episode exists. Existing and being discoverable are not the same thing.

This is where a lot of shows disappear. Not because they are bad. Not because the host has nothing to say. They disappear because nobody can figure out what they are, where they live, or why they should click.

That is not just an algorithm problem. That is a clarity problem.

## SEO Is Not Magic

SEO is not a secret trick. It is not stuffing the same phrase into your website forty-seven times. It is not naming every episode "Best Podcast for Podcasting Podcast Tips Podcast Growth Podcast Podcast." Please do not do that. That is not a title. That is a cry for help.

At its simplest, SEO means making your content easier for search engines to understand and easier for people to choose.

For show creators, this matters because audio by itself can be hard to discover. A listener may love your episode if they hear it, but Google, AI search tools, and regular humans need words around the episode to understand what it is.

If the only thing online is an audio file called "Episode 7," you are making the internet work too hard.

## Label the Box

Think of each episode like a box. Inside is the conversation, story, lesson, interview, laugh, argument, or moment. But the outside matters.

"Episode 12" tells me almost nothing. "Why New Podcasters Quit After Episode Six" tells me what is inside. "How to Choose Audio, Video, or Both Without Killing Your Show" tells me even more.

You are not tricking anybody. You are labeling the box.

## Every Episode Deserves a Page

If you want the show easier to find, every episode should have its own page. Not just a player. A page.

Include the title, summary, embedded audio/video, guest info, topics covered, links mentioned, transcript or recap, key takeaways, and one clear call to action.

This gives people something to scan before they commit. It also gives search engines and AI tools something to read. Search engines do not listen to your show the way people do. AI tools do not understand your story if it is trapped inside an audio file with no context.

Give the episode a written trail.

## Titles, Show Notes, and Transcripts

Do not name episodes like nobody is searching. Clever is fine, but clarity comes first. "Here We Go Again" could be anything. "Why New Creators Quit After Episode Six" tells me what I am getting.

Show notes are not filler. "This week we talk about stuff" is weak. A useful summary tells the listener what the episode covers and why it matters.

Transcripts are boring until they work. They make the show more accessible. They give search engines and AI tools text to understand. They help listeners skim. They give you material for clips, quotes, newsletters, and social posts.

A transcript turns spoken work into reusable written material.

## Links Are Trails

If you mention a guest, link to the guest. If you mention a resource, link to it. If you have a related episode, link to it. If a guest comes on your show, give them a clean link to share.

This is not just SEO. This is manners.

A show should not be a pile of disconnected episodes. It should become a little world. Links are how people move around that world.

## AI Search Makes This More Important

AI search does not make clarity less important. It makes clarity more important.

AI tools need understandable information. If your show has clear titles, useful descriptions, transcripts, guest pages, topic pages, and real experience behind it, you give people and machines a better chance of understanding what you do.

But do not write like a robot for the robots. The future does not belong to the person creating generic AI-friendly sludge. It belongs to the person creating useful, specific, human content that machines can understand without stripping away the soul.

## Topic Hubs

As the show grows, create topic pages: "Start Here," "AI Tools for Show Creators," "Better Interviews," "Audio, Video, or Both?" A topic hub tells people where to begin without digging through the archive like they are looking for a receipt from 2003.

Good discoverability is often just good hospitality.

## The Show Notes Template

A repeatable show notes template will save you.

Use one.

It might look like this:

Episode title.

One-sentence summary.

Why this episode matters.

Guest bio.

Three to five key takeaways.

Links mentioned.

Related episodes.

Transcript or recap.

One call to action.

That is enough.

Do not reinvent show notes every week.

Do not stare at a blank page after every episode like you are writing a college essay at 2:00 a.m. in 1991.

Make the template.

Fill it in.

Improve it over time.

## The Transcript Does Not Have to Be Perfect

A transcript can be raw, lightly cleaned, or polished.

Raw transcripts are useful for search and internal work, but they can be hard to read.

Lightly cleaned transcripts remove obvious errors, repeated false starts, and speaker confusion.

Polished transcripts read more like an article, but they take more time.

Pick the level that fits your workflow.

For many shows, a lightly cleaned transcript plus a strong summary is enough.

Do not let transcript perfection stop you from publishing.

Accessibility and discoverability matter, but sustainability matters too.

The transcript should help.

It should not become the reason the episode is three weeks late.

## Search Takes Time

Search is not instant.

This is frustrating because everything else online feels immediate.

You post something and refresh.

You upload something and check numbers.

You send an email and wonder why nobody replied in six minutes.

Search does not always work that way.

A page may take time to be discovered.

A topic hub may take time to matter.

A transcript may take time to help.

Internal links may take time to build a useful path.

That does not mean it failed.

It means you are planting.

The internet has enough fireworks.

Build something that can also be a garden.

I know that sounds too nice.

But it is true.

Search rewards bodies of work more than one desperate page most of the time.

Episode by episode, you are teaching the internet what your show is about.

## AI Search and Original Experience

AI search creates a new temptation.

Creators may start writing for answer engines instead of people.

That can make everything sound the same.

Do not do that.

AI tools can summarize common knowledge. What they cannot replace is original experience.

Your personal example.

Your guest's story.

Your local context.

Your mistake.

Your test.

Your opinion.

Your comparison.

Your "I tried this, and here is what happened."

That is valuable.

If you want your show to show up in a world full of AI summaries, do not become easier to summarize because you removed everything human.

Make your pages clear.

Make your structure useful.

But keep the lived experience.

That is the part worth finding.

## Internal Links Are Hospitality

Internal links are not just SEO.

They are hospitality.

If a listener lands on an episode about microphones, link to the episode about recording rooms.

If they land on an episode about naming, link to the cover art episode.

If they find a sponsor page, link to the best starter episode.

If they find the AI chapter, link to the show notes/transcript workflow.

You are building paths.

A person should not have to wander around your site like they are looking for customer service at a department store that closed in 2003.

Guide them.

Start here.

Listen next.

Related episode.

Sponsor info.

Guest form.

Newsletter.

That is good structure.

And good structure is kind.

## Closing Thought

Nobody owes your show discovery. You have to make it easier.

The episode is not done just because you exported the file. It is done when someone can find it, understand it, and decide whether it is for them.

# Chapter 12: Make the Show Feel Built

There is a difference between recording something and making a show. That difference is structure.

Not overproduction. Not fake radio voice. Not a bunch of sound effects flying around like somebody got a new toy and wants everyone to know it. Structure.

A show needs a beginning, a middle, and an end. It needs the listener or viewer to feel like someone thought about their time before they hit play.

## Conversation Is Not Enough

A conversation can wander. A show can breathe, but it should not wander forever. If you and a friend talk for ninety minutes, there may be a show in there. But the show may be the best forty-five minutes, or the best twenty, or the five-minute section where you finally got to the thing that mattered.

The listener does not owe you patience just because you recorded everything.

## The Opening Has a Job

The opening should tell people what they are about to hear, why it matters, and why they should stay. It can be funny, warm, direct, story-based, or a cold open from the best moment. But it should not waste time.

Do not warm up on the listener. Warm up before you record, or cut it later. If the real episode starts at minute seven, maybe the episode starts at minute seven.

Editing is not lying. Editing is mercy.

## Use a Repeatable Skeleton

A solo show might use: hook, why this matters, main idea, story, second point, practical takeaway, final thought, outro.

An interview show might use: guest welcome, why the guest matters, origin story, main challenge, turning point, lesson learned, listener takeaway, final question, outro.

A co-hosted show might use: cold open, welcome, topic setup, back-and-forth, recurring segment, listener question, takeaway, next episode tease, outro.

A skeleton does not kill creativity. It protects it.

## Interviews Need Preparation

A good interview is planned, not embalmed. Research the guest. Know why they matter to your audience. Know what you want from the conversation. Have questions ready, but do not become a prisoner of them.

Prep the road. Do not pour concrete over it.

If the guest says, "That was the year everything fell apart," do not move to question four. Ask, "What do you mean everything fell apart?" That is the doorway. Go through it.

Your question list is a map. It is not a pair of handcuffs.

## Talk Less, Host Better

A lot of hosts talk too much. We want to prove we know the topic. We want to prove the guest is in good hands. We want to prove we deserve the chair. So we talk. Then we ask a question that is actually a four-minute speech with a question mark stapled to the end.

That is not hosting. That is insecurity with a microphone.

A good host serves the show. Sometimes that means telling a story. Sometimes it means challenging the guest. Sometimes it means shutting up and letting the person finish the thought.

Silence is not always dead air. Sometimes it is useful air. Let the silence work.

## Endings Matter

A lot of shows just fall off the table. The guest says something good, the host says thanks, and the music wanders in like it got lost.

The ending is where the episode becomes a memory. Thank the listener. Anchor one takeaway. Point forward. Use a familiar sign-off.

The listener should feel like the show landed the plane, not like the pilot jumped out early.

## Opening Types You Can Use

Not every episode needs the same kind of opening, but every episode needs an intentional one.

Here are a few that work.

### The Promise Opening

Tell the audience exactly what they will get.

"Today we are going to help you decide whether your show should be audio, video, or both without turning your life into a production meeting."

### The Story Opening

Start with a small story that leads into the topic.

"The first time I heard my own voice recorded, I briefly considered becoming a silent partner in my own life."

**The Question Opening**

Ask the question the listener already has.

"What if the reason you have not started is not laziness, but a show that is too big to carry?"

**The Cold Open**

Use a strong moment from later in the episode, then bring people into the show.

This works especially well for interviews and story-driven episodes.

**The Contrarian Opening**

Challenge a common belief.

"More gear is not going to save your show. A simpler system might."

Pick the opening that fits the episode.

Just do not drift into it by accident.

## Segment Breaks Help the Listener

Segments are not only for radio.

They help the listener know where they are.

A segment can be simple.

"Here is where people get stuck."

"Let's talk about the setup."

"Now let's get practical."

"Here is the part nobody wants to hear."

Those little signposts matter.

They help the listener stay oriented.

They also help editing.

If you know the segments going in, you can see where the episode drifted.

You can move pieces.

You can cut repetition.

You can make the show feel built.

## Interview Follow-Up Lines

Good interviews often depend on follow-up questions.

Keep a few ready.

"What happened next?"

"How did you know?"

"What did that cost you?"

"What did people misunderstand?"

"When did you realize it was working?"

"What would you do differently now?"

"What are you leaving out because it feels obvious to you?"

"What did that feel like in the room?"

"What did you think was going to happen?"

"What surprised you?"

These questions are simple.

That is why they work.

They keep the guest in story and specifics.

Generic questions get generic answers.

Specific follow-ups open doors.

## Editing Passes

Do not try to fix everything in one edit.

Use passes.

First pass: structure.

Does the episode make sense?

Where does it really start?

What should be cut?

What needs to move?

Second pass: clarity.

Are there repeated points?

Do we need context?

Does the listener understand names, places, and references?

Third pass: pacing.

Does it drag?

Do the pauses help or hurt?

Is there a section that feels like walking through mud?

Fourth pass: technical cleanup.

Levels, noise, mistakes, weird clicks, music, intro, outro.

This sounds slower, but it is often faster than trying to hear everything at once.

Editing is where the recording becomes the show.

Respect that work.

## Outro Examples

A useful outro does not have to be complicated.

For a teaching show:

"Thanks for spending time with us. If there is one thing to take from today, it is this: do not build the biggest version first. Build the version you can repeat. Next time, we are going to talk about naming the show so people know what they found. Until then, start simple, tell the truth, and keep going."

For an interview show:

"Thanks to [Guest] for joining us, and thanks to you for listening. If this conversation made you think of someone, send it to them. That is how the right people find the show. We will be back next week with [tease]."

For a local show:

"If you have a story we should know about, send it to us at [email]. This show works because people remember things, notice things, and care enough to pass them on."

The outro should sound like the show.

But it should exist.

Do not Irish-goodbye your audience.

## Closing Thought

A show can be loose and still be built. It can be funny and still be structured. It can be emotional and still have a plan. Built does not mean stiff. Built means the listener can relax.

# Chapter 13: Be a Better Host

## Curiosity, listening, timing, follow-ups, ego, chemistry, and knowing when to shut up.

A lot of people think the host is the person who talks.

That is only partly true.

Yes, the host talks. If the host never talks, that is not a show. That is surveillance.

But talking is not the whole job.

The host is the guide.

That is the real job.

The host is the person who helps the listener know where they are, why they are there, what matters, when to lean in, when to laugh, when to think, when to move on, and why any of this was worth their time.

The host does not have to be the smartest person in the room.

Sometimes the host should absolutely not be the smartest person in the room.

The host does not have to know everything.

The host does not have to dominate.

The host does not have to turn every guest answer into a story about themselves.

The host does not have to perform wisdom like they are standing in front of a bookshelf on cable news.

A good host serves the show.

That sounds simple.

It is not.

Because the host has to do several things at once.

Listen to the guest.

Think about the audience.

Watch the clock.

Remember the outline.

Notice the better story.

Ask the follow-up.

Keep the energy alive.

Make the guest comfortable.

Challenge gently when needed.

Get out of the way when needed.

Land the plane.

And if it is video, also try not to look like they are reading a ransom note off the side of the screen.

Hosting is a skill.

You can get better at it.

You should get better at it.

Because a show can have a great concept, great guest, great equipment, and still fall apart if the host does not know how to guide the room.

## The Host Is the Listener's Representative

This is one of the best ways to think about the job.

The host represents the listener.

You are in the room, but you are not only there for yourself.

You are there for the person listening in the car, watching at lunch, folding laundry, walking the dog, driving across town, or sitting somewhere with headphones trying to make the day slightly more bearable.

That person cannot raise their hand.

You can.

They cannot ask, "Wait, what does that mean?"

You can.

They cannot say, "Go back to the part about your first business failure."

You can.

They cannot tell the guest, "You just used four acronyms and I do not know any of them."

You can.

That is hosting.

You are not only talking to the guest.

You are helping the audience stay in the conversation.

When a guest says something unclear, ask for clarity.

When a story jumps too far, bring it back.

When a subject gets too inside-baseball, translate.

When the guest gives a polished answer, ask for the real example.

When a conversation gets emotional, slow down.

When a topic gets complicated, summarize.

When a point lands, do not run over it like a lawn mower.

Let it breathe.

A good host is not just present.

A good host is useful.

## Curiosity Is Better Than Cleverness

Some hosts try too hard to sound clever.

They write complicated questions.

They stack four ideas into one question.

They make the question so long the guest needs a map and a snack to find the end of it.

Do not do that.

Curiosity is better than cleverness.

A simple, honest question can open a better door than a question trying to prove the host read three articles and wants credit.

“What happened next?”

“What did that cost you?”

“What did people misunderstand?”

“When did you know it was not working?”

“What did you do after the call ended?”

“What are you leaving out because it seems obvious to you?”

“Where were you when you realized things had changed?”

Those are not fancy questions.

They work.

Because they invite story.

A guest does not need the host to perform intelligence.

A guest needs the host to pay attention.

The audience does too.

## Shorter Questions Get Better Answers

This is painful, but true.

Shorter questions usually get better answers.

A lot of new hosts ask questions like this:

“So, I was thinking about how the industry has changed and how, especially after the pandemic, people had to rethink what they were doing, and then with AI and social media and all these new tools, it seems like people are kind of overwhelmed, but also there are opportunities, and I know in your case you had a business before and then you pivoted and now you are doing something different, so can you talk about that?”

That is not a question.

That is a pileup.

The guest may answer something, but who knows what.

Try this instead:

“When did you realize your old business model was not going to work anymore?”

That is a question.

Now the guest has a place to go.

Or:

“What changed after the pandemic?”

Or:

“What did AI force you to rethink?”

Or:

“What was the hardest part of starting over?”

One question at a time.

If you have three questions, ask the first one.

Then listen.

The other two may not matter anymore.

## Do Not Make the Guest Carry the Whole Thing

A guest can be interesting and still need help.

Some people are natural storytellers.

They know how to set up a scene, build tension, land a point, and make the audience care.

Others are not.

They may be brilliant but dry.

They may be nervous.

They may give short answers.

They may drift.

They may speak in résumé language.

They may promote instead of reflect.

They may think the audience knows more than they do.

Your job is to help.

That does not mean saving every weak answer by talking over them.

It means asking better follow-ups.

It means giving context.

It means saying, "For people who do not know that term, explain it."

It means asking, "Can you give me an example?"

It means asking, "What was that like in real life?"

It means asking, "What did that look like on a normal Tuesday?"

That last phrase is useful.

People can talk big concepts all day.

But "normal Tuesday" gets specific.

A good host helps the guest become more understandable.

And a great host helps the guest become more human.

## The Guest Is Not There to Read Their Bio

A lot of guests have a public version of themselves.

The bio.

The résumé.

The "About" page.

The LinkedIn version.

The clean, polished, sanitized version that makes everything sound more strategic than it felt at the time.

That version has a place.

But it is not always the best show.

The audience can read the bio.

They came for the conversation.

Your job is to get past the bio without being rude.

Instead of:

"Tell us about your career."

Try:

"What is the part of your career people misunderstand when they only read the bio?"

Instead of:

"How did you build your company?"

Try:

"What was the first moment where this became real and you realized you were responsible for it?"

Instead of:

"What are you proud of?"

Try:

"What did you have to learn the hard way?"

That is where the real show begins.

## Make the Guest Comfortable Before You Make Them Interesting

A nervous guest is usually not a great guest.

Some people can perform under pressure.

Most people need a minute.

Your job starts before the recording.

Send them a clear email.

Tell them what the show is.

Tell them how long it will take.

Tell them whether it is audio, video, or both.

Tell them how to prepare.

Tell them if you will ask about anything sensitive.

Tell them this is a conversation, not a trap.

Before you hit record, talk like a person.

Check sound.

Check video.

Make a small joke if that is your style.

Let them know you can edit if needed.

Tell them they can restart an answer.

Tell them if they stumble, it is fine.

Do not make the pre-record feel like they are checking into airport security.

The more comfortable the guest is, the more likely they are to tell the truth.

And truth is better than polished.

## Handling the Quiet Guest

Some guests are quiet.

They may be shy.

They may be thoughtful.

They may be nervous.

They may not know how much detail you want.

Do not punish them for that.

Ask narrower questions.

Instead of:

"Tell me about your childhood."

Try:

"What did Saturday mornings look like in your house when you were ten?"

Instead of:

"What was your career like?"

Try:

"What was your first real job where you thought, okay, I am an adult now?"

Instead of:

"How did you feel?"

Try:

"What did you do after you got the news?"

Specific questions help quiet guests.

Also, do not panic after a short answer.

Ask:

"Can you say more about that?"

Or:

"What do you mean by that?"

Or:

"Was that hard to say yes to?"

Quiet guests often open up when they realize you are actually listening.

Not waiting to move to the next question.

Listening.

## Handling the Guest Who Talks Too Much

Then there is the other kind.

The guest who talks in chapters.

You ask what time it is, and they explain the history of clocks, their childhood relationship with clocks, and why society has lost respect for punctuality.

Some people are talkers.

That can be great.

It can also bury the show.

You need tools.

First, use the setup.

"Today we have about forty minutes, so I may jump in to keep us moving."

That gives you permission.

Second, use the bridge.

"That is interesting, and I want to connect it back to..."

Third, use the summary.

"So the big turning point was the bank meeting. Let's stay there for a second."

Fourth, use the interruption politely.

"I am going to pause you there because that point is important."

Fifth, if needed, blame the audience.

"I want to make sure the listener has the context before we go too far."

That is not rude.

That is hosting.

The guest may not know they are going long.

Help them.

A good host protects the audience's time.

## Handling Emotional Moments

Sometimes a guest gets emotional.

This can happen suddenly.

A memory lands.

A loss comes up.

A regret appears.

A story they have told before hits differently this time.

Do not panic.

Do not make it about you.

Do not rush to fix it.

Do not say, "Wow, that's crazy," because apparently human beings say that when their brain cannot find a better sentence.

Slow down.

Let there be space.

You can say:

"Take your time."

Or:

"That sounds like it still carries a lot."

Or:

"I appreciate you saying that."

Or:

"We can pause if you want."

If the guest wants to continue, let them.

If they need a break, take one.

If the moment is too personal, ask later whether they are comfortable keeping it in.

Emotional moments can make a show powerful.

But they are not props.

Treat them with care.

## Handling Bad Answers

Sometimes the guest gives a bad answer.

Not morally bad.

Just weak.

Generic.

Boring.

Promotional.

Confusing.

This happens.

Do not accept it automatically.

Ask for an example.

"What is a real example of that?"

Ask for a story.

"When did you see that happen?"

Ask for the opposite.

"What do people usually get wrong about that?"

Ask for the hard part.

"What made that difficult?"

Ask for the cost.

"What did that cost you?"

Ask for the practical use.

"What should someone listening do with that?"

Often the first answer is the brochure.

The follow-up is the show.

## The Host's Ego Is Sneaky

Hosting can mess with your ego.

Sometimes the host wants to prove they belong.

They want to prove they know the topic.

They want to prove they are funny.

They want to prove the guest is lucky to be there.

They want to prove the audience should respect them.

That is normal.

It is also dangerous.

The host's ego can turn a good conversation into a tug-of-war.

You start talking too much.

You interrupt.

You top the guest's story.

You make the question about yourself.

You correct tiny things that do not matter.

You turn the episode into a performance of your own importance.

The audience feels that.

Tim Duncan — five championships, no highlights reel, no drama, just results — once said: "I don't try to change myself to impress anybody. I'm just who I am."

That is the model for this.

You do not have to be loud to hold the room.

You do not have to be flashy to run a good show.

You do not have to perform authority for the audience to trust you.

A confident host does not need to dominate.

A confident host can ask a short question and let the answer happen.

A confident host can say, "I do not know. Explain that."

A confident host can let the guest be brilliant.

A confident host can let the listener have the moment.

That is not weakness.

That is control.

## Do Not Make Every Story About You

This deserves its own section because we have all met this person.

Guest:

"My father died, and it changed everything."

Host:

"That reminds me of when my dog ran away for two hours in 1998."

No.

Not everything is your bridge.

There is a difference between connecting and hijacking.

A host story can help.

It can build trust.

It can make the guest feel safe.

It can show the audience why the topic matters.

But it should serve the conversation.

If your story takes the focus away from the guest at the wrong time, save it.

If your story makes the guest's vulnerability smaller, do not use it.

If your story is really just you wanting attention, be honest and let it go.

Good hosting often means resisting the urge to prove you have a related story.

You probably do.

That does not mean it belongs there.

## Chemistry With a Co-Host

Co-host chemistry is its own animal.

When it works, it is magic.

When it does not, it is two people trying to talk through the same doorway at the same time.

A co-hosted show needs rhythm.

One person sets up.

The other reacts.

One person tells the story.

The other asks the question.

One person pushes.

The other grounds.

One person brings facts.

The other brings feeling.

One person remembers the segment.

The other remembers the joke.

That is chemistry.

But chemistry is not just liking each other.

You can like each other and still make a bad show.

A good co-host helps the other host be better.

They do not compete for every laugh.

They do not correct every tiny detail.

They do not talk over every ending.

They do not bring the same energy every time.

They listen.

They toss.

They catch.

They build.

That is the dance.

And yes, I said dance.

No, I am not happy about it either.

## When to Challenge

A host should not be a jerk.

But a host also should not be a pillow.

Sometimes you need to challenge.

If a guest makes a big claim, ask for support.

If something does not make sense, ask for clarity.

If the audience would be skeptical, represent that.

If the guest is avoiding the real answer, gently bring them back.

If the topic is high-stakes, be careful.

Challenging does not mean attacking.

It can sound like:

"Help me understand that."

"Some people listening may push back on that. What would you say to them?"

"What evidence led you there?"

"What would you say to someone who tried that and it did not work?"

"Is there another side to that?"

That is useful.

You are not trying to win an argument.

You are trying to make the episode honest.

## When to Move On

A host also has to know when to move on.

Not every topic deserves ten more minutes.

Not every tangent is gold.

Not every guest story needs a follow-up.

Not every joke needs a callback.

Not every point needs to be repeated.

If the energy drops, move.

If the guest is repeating, move.

If the audience has enough, move.

If the episode promise is getting lost, move.

You can say:

"I want to shift to..."

"Let's move to the next piece."

"Before we run out of time, I want to ask..."

"That actually leads to something I wanted to cover..."

Those are simple tools.

Use them.

A show is not only what you include.

It is what you leave behind.

## Ending Like a Host

A host should know how to end.

Not just stop.

End.

A bad ending feels like everyone got tired and wandered off.

A good ending lands.

It summarizes what mattered.

It thanks the guest.

It gives the audience a next step.

It may tease what is next.

It leaves a feeling.

A good final question can help.

"What do you wish someone had told you at the beginning?"

"What is one thing you hope people take from your story?"

"What are you still learning?"

"What should someone listening do this week?"

"What did we not talk about that matters?"

Then close with intention.

Do not keep talking after the ending has arrived.

A lot of hosts miss the exit and circle the block three more times.

When you land it, land it.

## The Host's Prep Sheet

Before an episode, answer these questions.

What is the promise of this episode?

What does the audience need from the guest?

What is the one story I hope we get?

What is the one practical takeaway?

What should I avoid?

What is the sensitive territory?

What would make this episode worth sharing?

What question opens the door?

What question might create the best moment?

What is my closing question?

That prep does not make the show stiff.

It makes you ready.

A prepared host can be more spontaneous because they are not panicking.

## The Host's After-Action Review

After recording, review yourself.

Not like a bully.

Like a coach.

Did I listen?

Did I talk too much?

Did I ask short questions?

Did I interrupt?

Did I help the audience?

Did I let good moments breathe?

Did I miss a follow-up?

Did I make the guest comfortable?

Did I move on when needed?

Did the ending land?

Pick one thing to improve next time.

One.

Do not try to fix your entire personality between episodes.

That sounds exhausting and will probably involve snacks.

Pick one thing.

Get better slowly.

## Closing Thought

A host is not just the person with the microphone.

A host is the guide.

The listener is trusting you with their time.

The guest is trusting you with their story.

The show is trusting you with its shape.

That is the job.

Be curious.

Ask shorter questions.

Listen harder.

Follow the better story.

Know when to shut up.

Know when to step in.

Make the guest comfortable.

Make the audience feel included.

Land the plane.

You do not have to be perfect.

You do have to pay attention.

That is where better hosting begins.

# Chapter 14: Build the Machine Behind the Show

## Calendars, folders, checklists, templates, backups, show bibles, and the boring stuff that keeps the fun thing alive.

There is a part of making a show that nobody dreams about.

Nobody sits around as a kid thinking, “One day I hope to create a clean folder structure.”

Nobody stares out the window and says, “I just want to build a file-naming system that will make future me proud.”

Nobody watches MTV, old sitcoms, cable sports, late-night talk shows, radio dramas, or YouTube and thinks, “You know what really excites me? A guest intake form.”

But here is the annoying truth.

That boring stuff keeps the fun stuff alive.

The machine behind the show matters.

Not because creativity should become paperwork.

Not because we want to turn a show into a corporate operations manual with the personality of a printer jam.

Because every show eventually becomes a process.

And if the process is a mess, the show starts paying for it.

Files go missing.

Guests get confused.

Sponsors do not get what they were promised.

Episodes get delayed.

Clips never get made.

The website falls behind.

The host forgets what they already said.

The editor gets the wrong file.

The co-host thought they were recording Thursday, but you meant next Thursday, and now everybody is irritated and pretending they are not.

That is how shows die in the background.

Not with a dramatic explosion.

With friction.

Little friction.

Everywhere.

A show does not only need creativity.

It needs a machine.

Not a giant machine.

Not a cold machine.

Not one of those machines from an old factory movie where a man with a clipboard yells at everyone.

A simple machine.

A repeatable machine.

A machine that protects the show from your mood, your memory, your calendar, your tiredness, your inbox, your guests, your computer, and whatever life throws at you five minutes before record time.

That is what this chapter is about.

The boring stuff that keeps the good stuff going.

## Creativity Loves a Container

Some people resist systems because they think systems kill creativity.

I get that.

A checklist does not feel creative.

A production calendar does not feel creative.

A file naming convention does not feel creative.

But a system is not there to replace creativity.

It is there to protect it.

Think about television.

A sitcom had a format.

A drama had acts.

A radio show had segments.

A newspaper had sections.

A magazine had departments.

A music video had a runtime, a concept, a shoot day, an edit, and probably somebody dramatically leaning against a wall for no reason.

Structure has always been part of media.

The creative part lives inside the structure.

The problem is not having a system.

The problem is when the system becomes the boss and squeezes the life out of the thing.

We are not doing that.

We are building enough machine to keep the show moving.

That is all.

A good system should answer:

What happens next?

Where does this go?

Who needs this?

When is this due?

Has this been checked?

Can we find it later?

Those questions sound boring until you cannot answer them.

Then they become urgent.

## The Show Bible

Every show needs a show bible.

That sounds dramatic.

Like the show bible should be kept in a leather binder under glass with a little light shining on it.

It does not have to be fancy.

It can be a Google Doc.

A Notion page.

A Word file.

A printed folder.

A markdown file.

A notebook if you are the kind of person who can keep track of notebooks and not lose them in your car.

The show bible is the single place where the show's rules, identity, and process live.

It is not just for big productions.

It is especially useful for small shows because small shows usually rely on memory.

And memory is a liar with bad filing habits.

Your show bible should include:

Show title.

Subtitle.

One-sentence promise.

Audience.

Tone.

Format.

Episode length.

Publishing schedule.

Host bios.

Guest instructions.

Intro language.

Outro language.

Recurring segments.

Sponsor language.

Artwork rules.

File naming rules.

Folder structure.

Production checklist.

Publishing checklist.

Contact links.

Platform links.

AI prompts.

Sponsor packages.

Emergency plan.

That may sound like a lot.

It is.

But you do not have to build all of it on day one.

Start with the basics.

The point is not to create a museum of decisions.

The point is to stop re-deciding the same things every week.

## The One-Sentence Promise Belongs Everywhere

Your show bible should start with the one-sentence promise.

This is the spine.

Everything else hangs from it.

If the promise is:

"This is a show for people who remember the old media world and want to use new tools to finally tell their stories."

Then the machine should support that.

Guest choices.

Episode topics.

Artwork.

AI prompts.

Sponsor fit.

Website copy.

Clips.

Newsletter tone.

Everything.

When a decision gets weird, go back to the promise.

Should this guest be on?

Does it serve the promise?

Should we do this topic?

Does it serve the promise?

Should we add a new platform?

Does it serve the promise or just our fear of missing out?

The promise is not only marketing.

It is operations.

It keeps the machine from becoming random.

## Folder Structure: The Digital Junk Drawer Problem

Every creator eventually faces the digital junk drawer.

Files everywhere.

Downloads folder full of mystery audio.

Desktop covered in screenshots.

Final versions sitting beside final-final versions.

A guest headshot saved as "IMG_4827."

A sponsor logo somewhere in an email from three months ago.

An episode transcript named "transcript new one."

A video file so large your laptop makes a sound like it is considering legal action.

This is not sustainable.

You need a folder structure.

Not because you are trying to impress an IT manager.

Because finding things should not be a treasure hunt.

A simple show folder might look like this:

**Show Name**

- 00_Admin
- 01_Show_Bible
- 02_Episode_Planning
- 03_Guest_Assets

- 04_Raw_Recordings
- 05_Edits
- 06_Final_Exports
- 07_Show_Notes
- 08_Transcripts
- 09_Clips
- 10_Artwork
- 11_Sponsor_Assets
- 12_Reports
- 13_Archive

You can simplify that.

You can make it more specific.

But have something.

The goal is that anyone helping with the show can find what they need without texting you at 10:37 p.m. with "Where's the file?"

Because you will not enjoy that text.

And if you do enjoy that text, there may be other issues.

## File Naming: Boring Saves Lives

Okay, maybe file naming does not save lives.

But it saves episodes.

Use consistent file names.

Something like:

**ShowName_Ep001_GuestName_RawAudio_2026-07-12.wav**

**ShowName_Ep001_GuestName_Edit_v1_2026-07-13.wav**

**ShowName_Ep001_GuestName_FinalAudio_2026-07-14.mp3**

**ShowName_Ep001_GuestName_ShowNotes_2026-07-14.md**

**ShowName_Ep001_GuestName_Clip01_2026-07-15.mp4**

This looks nerdy.

Good.

Nerdy is useful.

The alternative is:

final.mp3

final2.mp3

realfinal.mp3

REALfinal_USETHIS.mp3

episode_mix_maybe_fixed.mp3

newnewnew.mp3

That is not a workflow.

That is a cry for help.

Pick a naming pattern.

Write it in the show bible.

Use it every time.

Future you will be grateful.

Future you is tired and just wants to upload the right file.

## The Production Calendar

A show needs a calendar.

Not just a vague feeling that episodes happen "weekly-ish."

A real calendar.

This does not mean you need project management software with fifteen views and a dashboard that looks like mission control.

It means you need to know:

When topics are chosen.

When outlines are due.

When guests are booked.

When recordings happen.

When edits are due.

When clips are due.

When show notes are due.

When the episode publishes.

When the newsletter goes out.

When sponsor reads are due.

When social posts go live.

For a weekly show, a simple calendar might be:

Monday: Finalize topic and outline.

Tuesday: Record.

Wednesday: Edit.

Thursday: Show notes, transcript, clips.

Friday: Publish and promote.

For a biweekly show, spread it out.

For a seasonal show, batch the whole thing.

The exact calendar does not matter as much as having one.

A calendar turns the show from "we should do something" into "this happens here."

That matters.

## The Buffer

A buffer is the space between production and panic.

Every show needs one.

If your episode is recorded the night before it publishes every single week, you are living dangerously.

Sometimes that is unavoidable.

News and sports shows may have tighter timelines.

Live shows are live.

But most shows can build a buffer.

One episode ahead is good.

Two is better.

A full season ahead is wonderful if the format allows it.

The buffer protects you when:

A guest cancels.

You get sick.

The edit takes longer.

The file corrupts.

Life happens.

A sponsor needs a change.

The website breaks.

Your computer updates itself at the worst possible moment because apparently it has dreams too.

Without a buffer, every small problem becomes a crisis.

With a buffer, problems are still annoying, but they are not always fatal.

Build the buffer.

Guard the buffer.

Do not spend the whole buffer unless you have to.

## The Episode Checklist

Every episode should go through a checklist.

Yes, every episode.

Because memory is not a system.

A basic episode checklist might be:

Topic chosen.

Episode promise written.

Outline created.

Guest booked, if any.

Guest confirmation sent.

Recording link sent.

Sponsor read confirmed.

Artwork or thumbnail prepared.

Recording completed.

Files saved and backed up.

Edit completed.

Audio levels checked.

Video export checked, if needed.

Title written.

Description written.

Show notes written.

Transcript created.

Links checked.

Episode uploaded.

Episode scheduled.

Website page published.

Newsletter drafted.

Clips created.

Social posts scheduled.

Guest share kit sent.

Sponsor notified.

Analytics recorded.

Archive updated.

That list may look long.

It is.

Making a show has more steps than people think.

The checklist is not there to make you feel overwhelmed.

It is there to get the steps out of your head.

A brain is a terrible place to store production details.

Use a checklist.

## The Recording Checklist

Before every recording, check:

Microphone selected.

Headphones working.

Recording platform open.

Storage space available.

Internet stable.

Camera framed, if video.

Lighting acceptable.

Notifications off.

Fan off.

AC noise checked.

Guest audio tested.

Guest video tested.

Guest has water.

Host has water.

Outline open.

Sponsor read ready.

Backup recording ready if needed.

Everyone knows the plan.

Record button actually pressed.

That last one is important.

Do not laugh.

At some point, every production person has either forgotten to press record or lived in fear of forgetting to press record.

Build the habit.

Say it out loud if you need to:

"We are recording."

The machine should protect you from the dumb mistakes.

Because the dumb mistakes are the ones that hurt the most.

## The Guest Tracker

If your show has guests, you need a guest tracker.

This can be a spreadsheet.

Keep track of:

Guest name.

Email.

Phone, if needed.

Topic.

Status.

Date invited.

Date confirmed.

Recording date.

Release date.

Bio received.

Headshot received.

Links received.

Release signed.

Prep email sent.

Thank-you sent.

Share kit sent.

Follow-up done.

Potential return topic.

Notes.

This may sound like overkill.

It is not.

Guest shows can become a scheduling swamp very quickly.

A tracker lets you see who is confirmed, who is pending, who ghosted you, who needs a nudge, and who gave you a headshot from 2007 that should probably not be used without a conversation.

It also helps you avoid booking the same kind of guest over and over.

If your show has variety, the tracker helps you see it.

## Guest Prep Saves Episodes

A good guest prep email saves time.

It should tell the guest:

What the show is.

Who listens.

Date and time.

Recording link or location.

Expected length.

Audio/video expectations.

What equipment they need.

Topics you expect to cover.

What they should send.

How the episode will be used.

Whether clips will be made.

When it will publish.

Who to contact with questions.

This is not just professionalism.

It is kindness.

Most guests want to do well.

Help them.

A prepared guest is more comfortable.

A comfortable guest is more useful.

A useful guest makes a better episode.

This is the machine serving the show.

## The Sponsor Tracker

If sponsors are involved, you need a sponsor tracker.

Please do not keep sponsor obligations in your head.

That is how you end up at 11:00 p.m. realizing the sponsor read was supposed to be in the episode that already published.

Track:

Sponsor name.

Contact.

Package.

Start date.

End date.

Episodes included.

Read length.

Script or talking points.

Links.

Promo code.

Logo.

Approval status.

Payment status.

Deliverables.

Publish dates.

Social posts.

Newsletter mentions.

Reports sent.

Renewal date.

Notes.

Sponsors are paying for reliability.

Be reliable.

A sponsor tracker is how you keep promises without turning your brain into a bulletin board.

## The Clip Tracker

If clips are part of your strategy, track them.

Episode.

Clip number.

Title.

Start and end time.

Platform.

Caption.

Status.

Post date.

Performance.

Notes.

This helps you learn what works.

Do teaching clips perform better?

Funny clips?

Guest stories?

Hot takes?

Emotional moments?

Local memories?

Sponsor clips?

Without tracking, you are guessing.

Guessing is fine at first.

Learning is better.

A clip tracker turns random posting into useful information.

And useful information helps you stop doing things that do not matter.

## The Show Notes Template

Do not write show notes from scratch every week.

Use a template.

A simple one:

Episode title.

Short summary.

Who this episode is for.

Key takeaways.

Guest bio.

Links mentioned.

Related episodes.

Transcript.

Call to action.

Sponsor note.

That is enough.

The template makes the process faster.

It also makes the website more consistent.

Consistency helps listeners.

It helps search.

It helps AI tools understand the archive.

It helps you not sit there wondering how to describe an episode you just spent three hours editing and now never want to hear again.

Use the template.

## The AI Prompt Library

If you use AI, build a prompt library.

Do not reinvent prompts every week.

Save the ones that work.

Episode outline prompt.

Guest research prompt.

Interview question prompt.

Transcript summary prompt.

Show notes prompt.

Clip finding prompt.

Title prompt.

Newsletter prompt.

Social post prompt.

Sponsor read prompt.

SEO description prompt.

Audience feedback prompt.

Put them in the show bible.

Label them clearly.

Update them when they improve.

A prompt library makes AI part of the machine.

Not a random toy you use when you are desperate.

And please remember:

AI drafts.

You decide.

The machine can help carry weight.

It does not get to drive the show into a ditch.

## Roles and Responsibilities

If more than one person touches the show, write down roles.

Do not assume everyone knows.

They do not.

Who books guests?

Who confirms the schedule?

Who records?

Who edits?

Who writes descriptions?

Who creates clips?

Who uploads?

Who checks links?

Who sends the newsletter?

Who talks to sponsors?

Who sends reports?

Who archives files?

Who makes final decisions?

This is especially important with friends, co-hosts, spouses, volunteers, interns, freelancers, or team members with overlapping jobs.

Unclear roles create resentment.

One person thinks the other person is handling it.

The other person thinks the first person is handling it.

Nobody handles it.

Then everyone is annoyed.

Write it down.

Not because you do not trust people.

Because you do not trust confusion.

## The Approval Process

Decide what needs approval and what does not.

Not everything needs a meeting.

Not everything needs three people to say yes.

But some things should be checked.

Sponsor reads.

Guest names.

Sensitive topics.

Final titles.

Thumbnails.

Legal concerns.

Claims.

Paid promotions.

High-stakes episodes.

If you have a team, define the approval process.

Who gets final say?

How long do they have?

What happens if they do not respond?

What can publish without approval?

If there is no process, everything becomes last-minute panic.

And last-minute panic is how mistakes sneak in wearing a fake mustache.

## Backups: The Unsexy Hero

Back up your files.

This should not need to be said, but it does.

Use cloud storage.

Use an external drive.

Use both if the show matters.

Save raw recordings.

Save final exports.

Save project files.

Save artwork.

Save transcripts.

Save sponsor assets.

Save contracts and releases.

Save the show bible.

If you lose an episode, that is bad.

If you lose the whole show archive, that is a crime scene.

Backups are boring until they are heroic.

Be boring.

## Version Control

Keep track of versions.

If an edit changes, name it.

If a script changes, name it.

If sponsor copy changes, save the approved version.

If artwork changes, archive the old one.

Do not let five versions float around with no idea which one is final.

This matters more as the show grows.

Version control prevents:

Wrong files going live.

Old sponsor reads being used.

Incorrect guest bios.

Unapproved artwork.

Confusing edits.

A final file should be clearly final.

Not final-ish.

Not "maybe this one."

Final.

## The Emergency Episode

Every show should have an emergency episode.

Something you can publish if the planned episode falls apart.

This might be:

A short solo episode.

A listener question episode.

A previously recorded evergreen episode.

A "best of" with new commentary.

A replay with an update.

A behind-the-scenes episode.

A short teaching episode.

A field note.

A bonus story.

The emergency episode keeps you from disappearing when the week goes sideways.

It does not have to be your best episode.

It has to be useful enough and ready enough.

Put one in the bank.

You may need it.

You will feel very smart when you do.

Enjoy that feeling. It is rare and should be appreciated.

## The Reset Plan

Sometimes the machine breaks.

The schedule slips.

The buffer disappears.

The folder structure becomes a junk drawer again.

The guest tracker is behind.

The show notes are late.

The team is tired.

This does not mean the show is dead.

It means you need a reset.

A reset plan might be:

Pause for one week.

Publish an emergency episode.

Clean the folders.

Update the tracker.

Record two evergreen episodes.

Simplify clips for a month.

Move to biweekly.

Drop one platform.

Rebuild the calendar.

Have a team meeting.

Send a clear note to the audience.

The reset is not failure.

It is maintenance.

Machines need maintenance.

So do people.

## The Metrics Log

Track basic numbers.

Not obsessively.

Usefully.

Episode title.

Publish date.

Downloads after 7 days.

Downloads after 30 days.

YouTube views.

Watch time.

Email opens.

Clip views.

Comments.

Shares.

Listener questions.

Guest referrals.

Sponsor clicks.

Whatever matters for your show.

Do not track everything just because you can.

Track what helps you decide.

Which topics connect?

Which guests bring the right audience?

Which clips work?

Which platforms matter?

Which calls to action move people?

A metrics log turns feelings into patterns.

Feelings are useful.

Patterns are better.

## The Meeting With Yourself

If you are a solo creator, have a meeting with yourself.

I know that sounds strange.

Do it anyway.

Once a week or once every two weeks, review:

What episode is next?

What is due?

What is stuck?

What needs to be simpler?

What needs follow-up?

What is working?

What is draining me?

What can I stop doing?

That last question is powerful.

What can I stop doing?

A lot of creators only add.

Add clips.

Add posts.

Add platforms.

Add guests.

Add segments.

Add newsletters.

Add sponsors.

Add pressure.

At some point, you need to subtract.

The machine should not grow until it crushes you.

## Team Check-Ins

If you have a team, hold a short production check-in.

Not a meeting that becomes a hostage situation.

A short check-in.

What is publishing next?

What is recording next?

Any guest issues?

Any sponsor issues?

Any files missing?

Any blockers?

Any decisions needed?

What is the priority?

That can be fifteen minutes.

A good check-in prevents a bad week.

Keep it focused.

End it.

Nobody gets an award for a long meeting unless they are billing by the hour, and even then, spiritually, they know.

## Document the Weird Stuff

Every show has weird stuff.

The intro music license.

The sponsor pronunciation.

The guest who only records on Mondays.

The platform that requires a special image size.

The editor's export settings.

The AI prompt that finally works.

The recurring segment rules.

The one phrase the host always says wrong.

The YouTube description template.

The newsletter subject style.

Document the weird stuff.

It may seem obvious now.

It will not be obvious later.

Especially if someone else helps.

A show bible full of weird practical knowledge is gold.

## The Machine Should Fit the Goal

A hobby show does not need the same machine as a business show.

A family legacy show does not need the same sponsor tracker as a local sports show.

A weekly video show needs a different machine than a six-episode audio fiction season.

Do not overbuild.

Build the machine that fits the show.

A hobby show might need:

Calendar.

Recording checklist.

Folder structure.

Simple publishing checklist.

A business show might need:

Lead tracking.

Sponsor assets.

Newsletter workflow.

Website pages.

Analytics.

A fiction show might need:

Scripts.

Cast list.

Sound design assets.

Continuity notes.

Release schedule.

A local show might need:

Guest tracker.

Community submissions.

Sponsor tracker.

Event calendar.

The machine should serve the purpose.

Not impress anyone.

## The Machine Should Be Easy to Use

If your system is too complicated, you will stop using it.

This is true of almost everything.

Exercise plans.

Budget spreadsheets.

Meal prep.

Project management systems.

That one app you downloaded because you thought it would organize your life and then never opened again.

Keep the machine simple enough that you will actually use it.

A messy system you use is better than a perfect system you abandon.

Start small.

Add only when needed.

The best machine is the one that disappears into the work.

It supports the show without demanding attention every five minutes.

## Closing Thought

The machine behind the show is not the glamorous part.

It will not get applause.

Nobody will leave a review saying, "Five stars, excellent folder structure."

But the machine matters.

It keeps the show from collapsing under its own little tasks.

It protects creativity.

It protects relationships.

It protects sponsors.

It protects your time.

It protects future you.

And future you needs all the help current you can give.

So build the machine.

The show bible.

The folders.

The calendar.

The checklists.

The trackers.

The templates.

The backups.

The emergency episode.

The reset plan.

Not because you love paperwork.

Because you love the show enough to keep it alive.

The fun thing deserves a boring machine behind it.

Build it.

Then get back to making the show.

# Chapter 15: Sound Like Yourself, Only More Intentional

At some point, you are going to hear yourself. Really hear yourself. Not the voice inside your head. The recorded version. The outside version. The version everybody else has apparently been hearing this whole time without warning you.

And for a lot of people, that is when the panic starts.

"Is that what I sound like?"

Welcome to the club.

Almost everybody hates their recorded voice at first. Your voice probably does not sound as bad as you think. It sounds unfamiliar. Those are not the same thing.

## The Outside Version

When you speak, you hear yourself partly through your own head. Vibration, resonance, bone conduction, all that strange human-body nonsense. A recording removes the inside version. So it sounds wrong.

It is not wrong. It is outside.

The audience is not hearing a disaster. They are hearing you. You are the one having the crisis.

## Your Voice Is an Instrument

Your voice is not a defect. It is an instrument. Instruments improve when you use them.

Do not put on a fake podcast voice. Do not suddenly become the guy from a monster truck commercial unless that is the actual show. The goal is not to sound like someone else. The goal is to sound like yourself, only more intentional.

Ice Cube — who has been exactly himself for about four decades straight — put it this way: "Nowadays, you can be yourself. You don't have to put on a façade. Reality is just as important as fiction."

He was talking about his career, but the idea holds here.

You are not performing a character.

You are not doing an impression of what you think a podcast host sounds like.

You are not auditioning for a version of yourself that seems more official or more polished or more worth listening to.

You are just you. Talking clearly. Saying the thing you actually think.

That is enough.

A little clearer. A little slower. A little more aware of the listener. A little more willing to pause. A little less afraid of your own sound.

## Listen Like a Coach, Not a Bully

The first listen is the worst listen because you are not just listening to the show. You are judging your whole existence.

A bully says, "This is terrible." A coach says, "The opening takes too long." A bully says, "You sound stupid." A coach says, "You sound more natural once you get to the story."

You need the coach. The world has enough bullies.

## Slow Down and Breathe

Most new hosts talk too fast. Nerves speed people up. Excitement speeds people up. Fear of silence speeds people up.

Slow down. Not painfully. Just enough that the listener can follow you.

Pauses are not the enemy. A pause can make you sound thoughtful, let a joke land, or give the listener time to catch up. The silence feels longer to you than it does to them.

Shorter sentences help too. When people get nervous, they stack thoughts until the listener is trapped inside a paragraph with no exits. Say one thing. Then say the next thing. That is not dumb. That is clean.

## Stop Apologizing Before You Start

"Sorry, I'm new at this." "Sorry, this may not be good." "Sorry, I'm rambling." Stop.

You can be honest without kneecapping the show before it begins. The listener clicked play. Let them decide.

## Practice Without Making It Precious

Record five minutes a day for a week. Do not publish it. Just practice. Tell a childhood story. Explain something you know. Review a movie you love. Talk about a mistake that taught you something. Practice asking interview questions. Record a fake opening and closing.

Then listen back and pick one improvement. One. Maybe you slow down. Maybe you stop apologizing. Maybe you pause more. Maybe you move the mic closer.

That is progress.

## Filler Words Are Not Crimes

You will say "um."

You will say "you know."

You will start sentences and restart them.

You will use some little verbal habit that makes you want to crawl under the desk when you hear it back.

Relax.

Filler words are not crimes.

They are part of speech.

The problem is not having any filler words.

The problem is when filler words make the listener work harder or make you sound unsure when you are not.

Do not try to remove every human sound.

That can make you sound edited by a robot with control issues.

Instead, notice the patterns.

Do you say "you know" when you are nervous?

Do you say "like" when you are searching?

Do you say "right?" after every point because you are asking for permission?

Do you laugh before saying something serious?

Do you trail off?

Pick one habit at a time.

Work on that.

Do not try to become perfect.

Perfect is not the goal.

Clear is the goal.

## Body Helps Voice

Your body affects your voice.

Sit or stand in a way that lets you breathe.

Do not fold yourself into a chair like a disappointed lawn chair.

Keep the mic close.

Keep your notes where you can see them without turning away from the microphone.

Take a breath before important points.

Drink water.

Warm up your mouth.

Read the opening out loud once before recording.

This is not theater kid nonsense.

It is practical.

If your body is tight, your voice may sound tight.

If you are hunched, rushed, thirsty, and staring at notes off to the side, the recording will tell on you.

A little physical preparation can make you sound more present.

## Video Presence Without Acting Weird

If you are on video, you do not have to perform like a morning show host who just won a blender.

You just need to look present.

Look at the guest when they are talking.

Look toward the camera sometimes when talking to the audience.

Do not stare at yourself the whole time.

You will start judging your face instead of listening.

Keep your background simple.

Keep your lighting good enough that people can see your eyes.

Sit in a way that looks awake.

Use your hands naturally if you normally do.

Do not freeze because you are on camera.

Video presence is not pretending.

It is letting the audience see that you are there.

## Listening Back Without Melting Down

Here is a listening plan.

First listen: only for structure.

Where does the show start?

Where does it drag?

Does the ending land?

Do not judge your voice yet.

Second listen: only for voice.

Do you talk too fast?

Do you sound like yourself?

Do you interrupt?

Do you apologize?

Third listen: only for technical issues.

Volume.

Echo.

Noise.

Mic distance.

Guest quality.

This keeps you from hearing everything as one giant blob of shame.

Separate the problems.

Fix one thing at a time.

That is how professionals improve.

Not by hating themselves.

By noticing.

## The Confidence Loop

Confidence does not usually show up before the work.

It shows up after enough repetition.

You record.

You listen.

You notice one thing.

You improve one thing.

You record again.

That is the loop.

At first, you may not feel confident.

That is fine.

Borrow structure until confidence arrives.

Use notes.

Use a skeleton.

Use an intro script.

Use a closing line.

Use a checklist.

Confidence grows when the process stops feeling mysterious.

You are not trying to become fearless.

You are trying to become familiar with the work.

Familiar is powerful.

## Closing Thought

Your voice is not the obstacle. Your fear of hearing it is.

Sound like yourself. Just a little clearer, slower, and more intentional. That is enough to begin.

# Chapter 16: The Thing That Makes People Quit

There is a point where the show stops being an idea and starts being work. That is where a lot of people disappear.

Not because they had nothing to say. Not because the idea was terrible. They quit because the thing got real.

At first, starting is exciting. Then the outline has to be written, the mic plugged in, the guest scheduled, the file edited, the title chosen, the description written, the clip made, and the post shared. After all that, the numbers may not be impressive.

That is when the voice starts: maybe this was a bad idea. Maybe nobody cares. Maybe I need better gear. Maybe I should research more. Maybe I should start over.

Sometimes that voice is useful. Sometimes it is fear wearing a blazer.

## Resistance Has a Microphone

Steven Pressfield calls this force Resistance. It shows up whenever meaningful work begins. It does not introduce itself. It sounds reasonable. It sounds like planning, research, waiting until things calm down, needing the perfect setup, or not wanting to embarrass yourself.

"I'm just not ready" is one of its best lines.

Preparation moves the show forward. Hiding keeps it safe in your head. A show in your head cannot fail. It also cannot help anybody.

## The Research Rabbit Hole

Research matters. But research can become a hole in the ground with Wi-Fi. At first you are learning. Then comparing. Then overthinking. Then watching one more gear review, testing one more AI tool, changing the name again, and somehow never recording.

Will this next piece of research change the next action? If yes, do it. If no, stop.

Research can inform you. Motion changes you.

## The Perfect Decision Trap

Perfect name. Perfect mic. Perfect camera. Perfect platform. Perfect artwork. Perfect launch date. Perfect first episode.

That sounds responsible, but it is a trap. Most creative decisions are working decisions. Choose a format for the first ten episodes. Use simple artwork and improve it later. Start audio-only and add video when the show proves it can survive.

The perfect decision is usually not available. The next honest decision is.

## Podfade Is Usually a System Problem

Podfade happens when excitement runs out and the system is not strong enough to carry the show. The cure is not always "try harder." Sometimes the cure is make the show easier to make.

Shorter episodes. Better outline. Batch recording. Fewer platforms. Simpler editing. Recurring segments. A season instead of weekly forever. A show bible. A checklist. A smaller version of the show.

There is no prize for building something that exhausts you.

## The Mountain Comes for Everyone

The Little Engine had a mountain. Every creator does too. Your mountain might be technology, self-doubt, money, time, editing, video, the sound of your voice, or embarrassment.

Do not assume the mountain means you are not supposed to do it. Maybe the mountain is just the mountain.

You do not need to be the biggest engine. You need to keep pulling.

## Bird by Bird, Show by Show

Anne Lamott's "bird by bird" idea is perfect here. You do not make the whole show at once. You make the next piece. Episode by episode. Segment by segment. Clip by clip. Question by question.

Shrink the assignment until it can move. Then move.

## The Launch High and the Launch Hangover

Launching feels good.

For about twelve minutes.

Maybe longer if people respond.

You announce the show.

Friends congratulate you.

Somebody says, "I've been thinking about starting one too," because apparently every creative announcement summons that sentence.

You get the first listens.

You feel official.

Then the next week shows up.

And the next episode is not theoretical anymore.

It needs to exist.

This is the launch hangover.

The applause was nice, but now the system has to work.

A lot of people do not plan for this.

They plan the launch.

They do not plan the second Tuesday.

Plan the second Tuesday.

That is where shows survive.

## Comparison Is a Thief With Good Wi-Fi

Comparison will mess you up.

You will look at someone else's studio.

Someone else's downloads.

Someone else's guests.

Someone else's thumbnails.

Someone else's confidence.

Someone else's sponsor.

Someone else's clips.

Someone else's audience.

And you will forget that you are looking at their current chapter while you are still writing your first few pages.

Do not compare your first episode to someone else's tenth year.

That is not ambition.

That is self-harm with analytics.

Use other shows for learning.

What do they do well?

What can you borrow structurally?

What do you not want to become?

What does their audience respond to?

That is useful.

But if comparison makes you freeze, close the tab.

The show is not made by staring at other people's progress.

## Public Promises and Private Systems

Public accountability can help.

Announcing a launch date can motivate you.

But a public promise without a private system is dangerous.

You need the behind-the-scenes plan.

When do you record?

When do you edit?

What if the guest cancels?

What if the episode runs long?

Who writes the show notes?

Where do files go?

What gets posted?

What gets skipped if time runs out?

The public sees the episode.

The private system makes it possible.

Build the private system before making too many public promises.

Or keep the public promise small.

Season one.

Ten episodes.

Every other week.

A pilot.

A limited series.

You can always grow the promise later.

## The Comeback Script

If you miss, come back simply.

Do not overexplain.

Do not make the return episode a guilt parade.

Say:

"We missed a week because life happened. We are back. Today we are talking about..."

That is enough.

The audience does not need you to perform shame.

They need a show.

If you need a break, name it.

"We are taking two weeks to finish the next batch of episodes. We will be back on [date]."

That is professional.

Disappearing without a word is what creates uncertainty.

Returning without drama is a skill.

Practice it.

## Resistance Near the Finish Line

Resistance gets loud near the finish line.

You recorded the episode.

Now you do not want to edit it.

You edited it.

Now you do not want to upload it.

You uploaded it.

Now you do not want to share it.

You made the website.

Now you do not want to send anyone there.

That is not random.

Publishing makes the work real.

Real work can be judged.

So Resistance says:

One more tweak.

One more delay.

One more week.

One more name change.

One more version.

Michael Jordan — who understood failure better than most people who talk about failure — said: "I can accept failure, everyone fails at something. But I can't accept not trying."

The episode sitting on your hard drive is not trying.

It is hiding.

Hiding feels safe. But a show in your head cannot fail, and it also cannot help anybody.

The version that gets published is the only version that can get better.

At some point, you have to publish.

Not because it is perfect.

Because it is ready enough to teach you what happens next.

Do not let the last ten percent become the graveyard.

## Closing Thought

The thing that makes people quit is not always failure. Sometimes it is fear before failure ever gets a chance. Make the work smaller, clearer, and more repeatable. Then make the next episode.

# Chapter 17: Don't Chase Everybody. Earn Somebody.

At some point, every show creator asks the growth question: how do I get more people to listen?

Fair question. But growth is where creators lose their minds. They start chasing everybody. Everybody to listen, watch, share, subscribe, review, care.

That is not a strategy. That is panic with a login.

You do not need everybody. You need the right people.

## Attention Is Not Audience

A clip gets a bunch of views but nobody listens. A post gets likes from people who never come back. A paid ad gets clicks but no one stays. That can look good and build nothing.

Attention is not audience. Reach is not relationship. A view is not trust. A download is not loyalty.

Ice Cube said it straight: "Don't worry about being a star, worry about doing good work, and all that will come to you."

That is the whole chapter in one sentence.

Not: chase the numbers and hope the work follows.

The other way around.

Do the work that matters to the right people. Do it consistently enough that the right people start coming back. Then do it again.

The star part — if it comes — comes from that. Not from chasing it.

If you are building for the long haul, you are trying to become worth returning to.

## 1,000 True Fans and the First Ten

The "1,000 True Fans" idea matters here. A creator does not necessarily need millions of casual followers. A smaller group that truly cares can build something real.

But before 1,000, find ten.

Ten real people who are close enough to the audience to tell you whether the show works. Not bots. Not random likes. Not people who hate the topic. The right ten.

Ask useful questions: What did you think the show was about? Where did you get interested? Where did you drift? What would you want more of? Would you listen again? Who would you send this to?

## People Share Moments

People do not usually share an episode because the topic is generally good. They share a moment. A line. A story. A joke. A hard truth. A useful explanation. A moment where the guest finally says the thing.

If you want growth, build episodes that create moments. Ask better questions. Tell better stories. Give specific examples. Say the hard truth plainly.

AI can help find the moment. It cannot create one from mush.

## Promotion Is Not Begging

Promotion can feel gross, like clanging a spoon in a restaurant and announcing that you made content. But promotion is not begging if the episode is useful.

Promotion is helping the right people find the thing you made for them.

Do not just say, "New episode is out." Tell people why it matters. "If you are putting off your show because gear feels overwhelming, start here." That gives someone a door.

## One Clear Ask

Every episode should have one clear call to action. Not seven. Follow the show. Join the email list. Send a question. Share this with one person.

One clear ask is stronger than a grocery list of desperation.

## The Algorithm Is Weather

Social platforms can help. Clips can help. Guest tags can help. But social media is distribution, not religion.

The algorithm is not your audience. It is a weather system. Build for people.

## The Audience Ladder

Think of audience growth as a ladder.

At the bottom is awareness.

Someone sees a clip, hears about the show, or gets sent a link.

Next is sampling.

They try an episode.

Next is return.

They come back.

Next is trust.

They start believing the show is worth their time.

Next is participation.

They comment, email, ask a question, or share a story.

Next is advocacy.

They tell other people.

Next is support.

They buy, sponsor, attend, join, donate, subscribe, or otherwise help sustain the show.

Do not ask people to jump to the top of the ladder before they have stepped on the first rung.

A stranger may not buy merch.

But they might watch a clip.

A first-time listener may not join a membership.

But they might follow.

A regular listener may not sponsor you.

But they might send the episode to a friend.

Respect the ladder.

Build the next step.

## Make Sharing Easy

If you want people to share, help them.

Give clean episode links.

Give short descriptions.

Give guests share copy.

Give clips with captions.

Give a sentence people can use.

Most people are busy.

They may like your show and still not know how to describe it.

Do not make them work.

After a guest episode, send:

The episode link.

Two or three clips.

A short caption.

A quote card if useful.

A thank-you note.

That is not pushy.

That is helpful.

The easier you make sharing, the more likely it happens.

## Collaborations Beat Cold Shouting

One of the best ways to find listeners is through people who already have trust with them.

Other shows.

Newsletters.

Local groups.

Facebook communities.

Business organizations.

Churches.

Schools.

Clubs.

Events.

Creators.

Guests.

This is why cross-promotion can work.

You are not yelling at strangers.

You are being introduced.

Find shows or communities that serve a similar audience but are not direct copies of yours.

Offer value.

Do not just ask for attention.

Can you guest on their show?

Can you swap trailers?

Can you share a useful guide?

Can you invite them on?

Can you create a joint episode?

Can you mention them honestly?

Relationships grow shows better than cold shouting most of the time.

## The Comment Is Content

Audience responses are not just feedback.

They can become part of the show.

Listener questions.

Corrections.

Stories.

Follow-ups.

Examples.

Disagreements.

Memories.

Recommendations.

These can all become segments.

This is how a show starts feeling alive.

Not because the audience controls it.

Because the audience knows they matter.

A listener who hears their question answered may become a loyal listener.

A local story submitted by one person may bring in ten more.

A comment that challenges you may create a better episode.

Do not ignore the people who are already leaning in.

They are showing you where the show has a pulse.

## Do Less, Better

Growth plans often get too big.

Post daily.

Make clips.

Start a newsletter.

Run ads.

Guest on shows.

Build a Facebook group.

Do live streams.

Create a Discord.

Make merch.

Launch a Patreon.

Please breathe.

Pick the growth actions you can actually repeat.

For the first ten episodes, maybe it is:

One good episode page.

One email.

Two clips.

One guest share kit.

One clear call to action.

One listener feedback question.

That is enough to start.

Do less, better.

Then add more when the system can hold it.

## Closing Thought

Do not chase everybody. Earn somebody. Then earn the next somebody.

Behind every download, view, comment, email, share, and subscription is a person who gave you a little piece of their time. Treat that like it means something.

# Chapter 18: Launch Without Making It Weird

## Trailers, first episodes, soft launches, hard launches, first 30 days, and why refreshing the numbers every six minutes is not a growth strategy.

Launching a show feels bigger than it is.

I do not mean it is not important.

It is important.

But people make launch day into this giant emotional event where the whole future of the show is apparently going to be decided by whether sixteen people click the link before lunch.

That is too much pressure.

That is how people turn a perfectly good creative project into a little nervous breakdown with cover art.

The launch matters.

But the launch is not the show.

The launch is the door opening.

That is it.

The show is what happens after people walk in.

A lot of creators get this backward. They spend months building up to the launch like they are releasing a blockbuster movie in 1997. They announce. They tease. They redesign the logo twelve times. They make a trailer. They build a countdown. They tell everybody they know. They get nervous. They imagine people listening. They imagine nobody listening. They imagine success. They imagine public humiliation. They imagine their old high school friend hearing it and thinking, "Well, that was certainly a choice."

Then launch day comes.

They post the link.

They get a few comments.

Maybe some downloads.

Maybe a nice text from somebody.

Maybe nothing dramatic.

And then they wake up the next day and realize something horrifying.

They still have to make the next episode.

That is the part nobody puts in the launch graphics.

A launch is not the finish line.

A launch is the beginning of the job.

So let's make it less weird.

Let's launch in a way that gives the show a chance to grow without making you feel like you are standing on a stage in your underwear while holding a microphone you are not sure is turned on.

## First, Decide What Kind of Launch This Is

Not every show needs the same kind of launch.

Some shows should be launched quietly.

Some should be launched loudly.

Some should be tested first.

Some should release as a full season.

Some should launch with a trailer.

Some do not need a trailer.

Some should start with three episodes.

Some should start with one.

Some should begin as a private pilot.

Some should go public quickly because the topic is timely.

The mistake is thinking there is one correct way.

There is not.

There is only the launch that fits the show, the creator, the audience, and the amount of energy available.

Before you announce anything, decide what kind of launch you are doing.

Are you testing?

Are you building an audience from scratch?

Are you bringing over an existing audience?

Are you launching a business-facing show?

Are you launching a fiction or documentary season?

Are you launching a local show where personal relationships matter?

Are you launching a YouTube-first show where clips and thumbnails matter?

Are you launching audio-only and adding video later?

Different answers create different launch plans.

Do not copy someone else's launch without knowing what game they were playing.

That is how people end up doing a bunch of work that makes no sense for their show.

## The Private Pilot

A private pilot is an episode you record before you launch and share with a small group of trusted people.

This can be extremely useful.

Especially if you are nervous.

Especially if the show is new.

Especially if you are still figuring out format.

Especially if the idea is strong but the execution is untested.

A private pilot lets you learn before the whole thing is public.

You can test the sound.

Test the structure.

Test the length.

Test the host chemistry.

Test whether the show promise is clear.

Test whether people understand what they are hearing.

Test whether you can actually make the thing.

This is not cowardice.

This is smart.

Television has pilots.

Businesses test products.

Restaurants do soft openings.

Bands rehearse before playing.

Even your uncle who plays "Sweet Home Alabama" at every family gathering probably practiced at some point, though evidence may vary.

A private pilot is rehearsal with purpose.

Send it to a small group of people who are close to the audience.

Not just people who love you.

People who can give useful feedback.

Ask them:

What did you think the show was about?

Where did you get interested?

Where did it drag?

What confused you?

Would you listen to another episode?

Who would you send this to?

What moment stuck with you?

Do not ask only, "Did you like it?"

People are too nice.

Or too weird.

Either way, "Did you like it?" is not enough.

You need useful feedback.

## The Soft Launch

A soft launch is when you release the show without making a huge public announcement yet.

This can be great.

A soft launch gives you a chance to make sure everything works.

The RSS feed works.

The show appears in the major apps.

The YouTube playlist is clean.

The website links are correct.

The episode pages look right.

The audio file is not accidentally the wrong version.

The guest's name is spelled correctly.

The show description does not contain a typo that makes you look like you typed it while being chased.

This is also when you can invite your first ten or twenty people to listen and give feedback.

A soft launch might be:

"Hey, I quietly put the first episode up. I'm testing the show before I announce it publicly. Would you listen and tell me what you think?"

That is a soft launch.

Low drama.

Useful.

The goal is not to make a splash.

The goal is to make sure the pool has water in it before you jump.

## The Hard Launch

A hard launch is the public announcement.

This is where you tell people:

The show exists.

Who it is for.

Why it matters.

Where to find it.

What to do next.

This can be exciting.

It can also be awkward.

Because now you have to tell people you made something.

For some of us, that is weird.

We can talk all day about other people's projects. But when it is ours, suddenly we become humble in the least useful way.

"Oh, it's nothing."

"It's probably not very good."

"I'm just messing around."

"I don't know if anybody will care."

Stop that.

Do not apologize for the show in the announcement.

You do not have to brag like you just invented electricity.

But you should be clear and proud enough to let people know what you made.

The announcement should say:

I made this.

This is who it is for.

This is why I made it.

Here is where you can listen or watch.

Here is the one thing I would love for you to do.

That is enough.

## Do You Need a Trailer?

Maybe.

A trailer can be useful.

It gives people a quick way to understand the show.

It gives podcast apps and platforms something to display before the first full episode.

It gives you a short link to share.

It helps you say the promise out loud.

It can make the show feel real.

But a trailer is not mandatory for every show.

If making the trailer becomes another reason to delay launching, skip it.

If you already have a clear first episode, you can launch with that.

If your show is seasonal, documentary, or audio fiction, a trailer may matter more because it sets tone and expectation.

If your show is an interview or teaching show, a trailer can still help, but it does not need to be some cinematic masterpiece.

A simple trailer can be sixty to ninety seconds.

Who are you?

What is the show?

Who is it for?

Why does it matter?

When does it launch?

Where can people follow?

That is it.

You do not need thunder sounds unless the show requires thunder sounds.

And even then, use thunder responsibly.

## Trailer Structure

A simple trailer structure:

10. Start with the problem or feeling. 2. Introduce the show. 3. Say who it is for. 4. Say what people will get. 5. Give the release schedule. 6. Tell people where to follow.

Example:

"Maybe you have had a show idea sitting in your head for years, but every time you get close to starting, the tools, gear, platforms, and your own self-doubt get in the way. This is *Start Simple, Tell the Truth, Keep Going*, a show for people who remember the old media world and want to use new tools to finally make something real. We will talk about show ideas, gear, story, AI, video, sponsors, consistency, and how to build the version you can actually keep making. Follow now wherever you listen or watch, and start with us on [date]."

That is a trailer.

It is not trying to win an Oscar.

It is trying to open the door.

## How Many Episodes Should You Launch With?

This is another question people overthink.

There is no perfect number.

Launching with one episode is fine.

Launching with two or three can be better for some shows.

Launching with a full season may be right for fiction or documentary.

Here is how I would think about it.

If the show is ongoing and weekly, launch with one trailer and one full episode, or with two full episodes if you can.

If you want people to sample more than one version of the show, launch with three episodes.

If the show is interview-based, three episodes can help show range.

If the show is seasonal or narrative, consider having the full season recorded or at least most of it ready before launch.

If the show is audio fiction, do not launch with one episode and then disappear for two months unless your goal is to hurt people emotionally.

That is not suspense.

That is abandonment.

The real question is not only how many episodes to launch with.

The real question is:

How many episodes can you keep making after launch?

Do not burn your whole buffer on day one if it leaves you panicking by week two.

A launch batch is good.

A survival buffer is better.

## The First Three Episodes

If you launch with three episodes, make them intentional.

Do not just release the first three things you recorded.

Use them to show the range and promise of the show.

Episode one should explain the core promise.

Episode two should show the show in action.

Episode three should prove there is more road ahead.

For a creator show, that might be:

Episode 1: Why Your Voice Still Matters

Episode 2: What Are You Actually Making?

Episode 3: Don't Build a Studio Before You Build a Habit

That gives emotional reason, clarity, and practical help.

For a local history show:

Episode 1: Why Forgotten Places Matter

Episode 2: The Diner Everyone Still Talks About

Episode 3: How the Highway Changed the Town

Now the audience understands the mission, hears a story, and sees the bigger theme.

For a business show:

Episode 1: The Problem We Solve

Episode 2: A Real Example

Episode 3: The First Practical Framework

That is a smart launch.

The first few episodes are not just content.

They are the welcome mat.

## The Launch Checklist

Before you announce publicly, check the basics.

Show title final enough?

Subtitle or description clear?

Cover art readable at small size?

Trailer or first episode uploaded?

Podcast apps connected if audio?

YouTube playlist ready if video?

Website or home base working?

Episode pages live?

Newsletter signup working?

Social profiles updated?

Guest links correct?

Sponsor mentions correct if any?

Transcript or show notes ready?

One main link ready to share?

Call to action clear?

Test the links.

Seriously.

Click them.

On your phone.

On a computer.

In an incognito window if needed.

Ask somebody else to click them.

Nothing makes launch day more annoying than telling everyone to go to a link that does not work.

That is the kind of thing that makes you want to walk quietly into the woods and become a rumor.

Check the links.

## Your One Main Link

For launch, you need one main link.

Not twelve.

One.

A website page is best if you have it.

That page can include buttons for Apple, Spotify, YouTube, email signup, and other platforms.

If you do not have a website yet, use the best central link you have.

But do not make people choose from a pile of links in your announcement.

The announcement should be simple.

Go here.

Listen or watch.

Follow.

Share with one person.

That is enough.

People are busy.

Do not make them solve your distribution puzzle.

## The Launch Announcement

Your launch announcement should sound like you.

Not like a press release got trapped inside a LinkedIn post.

You can write it simply.

Something like:

"I finally made the thing I have been talking about making. It is called [SHOW NAME], and it is for [AUDIENCE]. We are talking about [TOPIC/PROMISE]. If you have ever [PROBLEM/FEELING], I think this is for you. The first episode is live now. You can listen/watch here: [LINK]. If it connects with you, follow the show and send it to one person who would get something out of it."

That works.

It is human.

It tells people what to do.

It does not apologize.

It does not overhype.

It does not promise that this show will change the entire future of media, which is good because that is a lot to ask of episode one.

## Launch Email

If you have an email list, use it.

If you do not, send personal emails to the first people who should know.

Do not blast a giant impersonal message to everyone you have ever met unless that actually makes sense.

A personal note works better.

"Hey, I wanted you to know I launched the show I have been working on. It is about [promise], and I thought of you because [specific reason]. I would love for you to listen to the first episode and tell me what stuck with you."

That is much better than:

"Dear valued contact, I am excited to announce..."

No.

Do not sound like a bank merger.

Sound like a person.

## Social Posts Without Feeling Gross

Social posts feel weird because you are basically saying, "Look at this thing I made."

But that is not wrong.

You did make a thing.

If you believe the thing is useful, share it.

The key is to make the post about the reader, not just your feelings.

Weak launch post:

"My new podcast is live! Please listen!"

Better:

"If you have had a show idea sitting in your head but keep getting stopped by gear, fear, AI, video, or not knowing where to start, I made this for you. The first episode of [SHOW NAME] is live now."

That gives someone a reason.

You can still say you are excited.

You should.

Just do not make the whole post an emotional weather report.

Tell people what they get.

## Asking for Reviews

Reviews can help, depending on the platform.

But asking for reviews too early can feel awkward if nobody has had time to decide whether the show is good.

Instead of immediately begging for reviews, start with following and sharing.

Early ask:

"If this feels like something you want more of, follow the show so you get the next episode."

Second ask:

"If this episode made you think of someone, send it to them."

Later ask:

"If you have been listening and the show has helped, a rating or review would mean a lot and helps other people find it."

That is a reasonable progression.

Do not ask a person to write a review before they know what they think.

That is like asking someone to review a restaurant before the food arrives.

## Your First Thirty Days

The first thirty days are not about becoming famous.

They are about learning.

That is the mindset.

You are watching what happens when the show meets the world.

Do people understand the title?

Do they understand the promise?

Which episode gets the most response?

Where do people click?

What do they say?

What questions do they ask?

What confuses them?

What do guests share?

What clips work?

What posts feel natural?

What parts of the process are too heavy?

What did you underestimate?

This is research.

Real research.

Not theoretical research.

The kind that comes from doing the thing.

Do not waste the first thirty days refreshing numbers and feeling weird.

Use them.

## Week One: Make Sure It Works

In week one, your job is to make sure the show is findable and playable.

Check platforms.

Check the website.

Check links.

Check audio quality.

Check video playback.

Check descriptions.

Check artwork.

Check the email signup.

Check that the episode page makes sense.

Reply to people who comment or message.

Thank the first listeners.

Do not obsess over numbers yet.

The first week often reflects who already knows you, not what the show can become.

It is not the whole story.

It is the first page.

## Week Two: Ask for Useful Feedback

In week two, reach out to a small group of the right people.

Ask useful questions.

What did you think the show was about?

Where did you get interested?

Where did it drag?

Would you listen again?

Who would you send it to?

What moment stuck?

Collect the answers.

Do not defend everything.

Do not argue.

Do not explain the show for ten minutes if they did not understand it.

That is the feedback.

If you have to explain the show after they heard the show, something may need to be clearer.

Thank them.

Then look for patterns.

One person's opinion is an opinion.

Three people saying the same thing is information.

## Week Three: Share Better Moments

In week three, focus on moments.

Look at the episode or episodes and find the strongest clips, quotes, stories, or takeaways.

Share those.

Do not just keep posting "new episode out."

Find the piece that might make someone care.

The funny line.

The useful framework.

The emotional moment.

The surprising point.

The guest story.

The before-and-after.

The clip is the doorway.

Make it a good doorway.

## Week Four: Review and Adjust Lightly

In week four, review.

Not dramatically.

No giant identity crisis.

Ask:

Did the launch work technically?

Did people understand the show?

What got the strongest reaction?

What confused people?

Did the format feel sustainable?

What took too long?

What was easier than expected?

What should we keep for the next four episodes?

What should we adjust?

The key word is lightly.

Do not change the whole show after thirty days because the numbers were smaller than your fantasy.

Fantasies are terrible benchmarks.

Make smart adjustments.

Then keep going.

## What Not to Panic About

Do not panic if the numbers are small.

New shows start small.

Do not panic if your friends do not all listen.

Some will not. That is fine.

Do not panic if someone says, “I have not had time yet.”

They may mean it.

Do not panic if one platform performs better than another.

That is useful information.

Do not panic if your first clip does nothing.

Post another one.

Do not panic if you hate the sound of one section.

Make the next one better.

Do not panic if the launch feels quieter than expected.

A quiet launch can still lead to a strong show.

The launch is not the verdict.

It is the start.

## What to Actually Measure

Measure things that help you make decisions.

Can people find it?

Are people playing it?

Are people finishing it?

Are people following?

Are people responding?

Are people sharing?

Which episode or clip got the most useful reaction?

Which platform seems to fit?

How long does production take?

Can you keep the schedule?

Did the audience understand the promise?

Those are useful.

Checking downloads every six minutes is not useful.

That is not analytics.

That is emotional roulette.

Set a time to check numbers.

Maybe once a week at first.

Write them down.

Look for trends.

Then go make the next episode.

## The Launch Is Not the Best Episode

Your launch episode may not be your best episode.

That is okay.

In fact, it probably should not be.

If episode one is the best thing you ever make, that is a sad little creative career.

The point is to improve.

The first episode needs to be good enough to represent the show and useful enough to respect the listener.

It does not need to be perfect.

You will get better.

Your openings will tighten.

Your voice will settle.

Your structure will improve.

Your editing will get cleaner.

Your audience understanding will sharpen.

Your titles will get better.

Your clips will get stronger.

Your confidence will become less fragile.

That only happens after launch.

You cannot become experienced before doing the thing.

Annoying, but true.

## Guests During Launch

If guests are involved in your launch, make sharing easy for them.

Do not just send:

“Episode is live!”

Send a small share kit.

Include:

Episode link.

Short description.

Two or three suggested social captions.

A quote or clip.

Any artwork.

A thank-you.

Make it easy.

Guests are busy.

They may want to share but not know what to say.

Give them the tools.

Also, tell them when the episode is going live before it goes live.

Nobody likes being surprised by their own face on the internet before coffee.

## Sponsors During Launch

If you have a launch sponsor or founding sponsor, be especially organized.

Confirm the read.

Confirm the links.

Confirm the dates.

Confirm the deliverables.

Send the episode when it goes live.

Send the clips or screenshots.

Track the basic numbers.

Send a short recap.

This is how you build trust with sponsors.

Even if it is a free trial or discounted founding sponsorship, treat it professionally.

Practice like money is already involved.

Because eventually, you want it to be.

## The Launch Mistakes

Here are common launch mistakes.

Waiting too long.

Launching with no clear promise.

Launching with broken links.

Launching with artwork nobody can read.

Launching with one episode and no plan for the next one.

Launching with too many platforms and no workflow.

Launching without telling anyone.

Launching by telling everyone but giving them no reason to care.

Launching and then immediately apologizing for the show.

Launching and then changing everything after one week.

Launching and then disappearing.

All fixable.

But easier to avoid.

## The "Ready Enough" Standard

You need a ready-enough standard.

Not perfect.

Ready enough.

Ready enough means:

The episode represents the show.

The audio is listenable.

The title is clear.

The description makes sense.

The main link works.

The next episode is planned.

The call to action is simple.

The show is not embarrassing because of laziness.

That last part matters.

There is a difference between imperfect and careless.

Imperfect is allowed.

Careless is not.

A first episode can be rough.

It should not be sloppy in ways you already know how to fix.

Respect the listener.

Then publish.

## Launch Energy vs. Show Energy

Launch energy is loud.

Show energy is quieter.

Launch energy says:

"Everybody look!"

Show energy says:

"Let's make the next good episode."

You need both.

But if I had to pick, I would rather have show energy.

A big launch with no follow-through is a firework.

A steady show with clear value is a campfire.

Fireworks are exciting.

Campfires keep people around.

Build the campfire.

## The First 90 Days

The first thirty days are learning.

The first ninety days are shaping.

By ninety days, you should know more about:

Your production rhythm.

Your audience.

Your strongest topics.

Your weakest workflow points.

Your platform fit.

Your show length.

Your clip strategy.

Your guest process.

Your own energy.

Your realistic schedule.

That does not mean everything is solved.

It means the show is no longer imaginary.

That is a huge win.

A lot of people never get there.

If you make it ninety days, review the show seriously.

Should you keep the same format?

Should you change frequency?

Should you add video?

Should you simplify?

Should you build sponsor materials?

Should you create a newsletter?

Should you plan a season break?

Should you double down on a certain topic?

Should you stop doing something that is not working?

That is the review.

Do it after real data.

Not after one weird Tuesday.

## Launch Again

Here is a useful idea.

You can launch more than once.

You can launch the trailer.

Launch episode one.

Launch season two.

Launch the video version.

Launch the newsletter.

Launch the live show.

Launch a sponsor campaign.

Launch a limited series.

Launch a better website.

Launch a new segment.

Launch an anniversary episode.

You do not get only one chance.

That should take some pressure off.

The first launch matters, but it is not the only doorway.

If you learn and improve, you can create new moments for people to find the show.

That is another reason not to make the first launch too precious.

It is a beginning.

Not your one shot at the moon.

## A Simple Launch Plan

Here is a simple plan for a new show.

Two to four weeks before launch:

Record a private pilot.

Get feedback.

Finalize name, artwork, and show description.

Set up hosting, YouTube if needed, website or landing page, and email signup.

Record the first two or three episodes if possible.

One week before launch:

Upload trailer or first episode privately.

Test links.

Prepare launch post and email.

Prepare guest share kits if needed.

Create one main launch page.

Launch day:

Publish the episode.

Send the email.

Post on main social channels.

Message first ten people personally.

Reply to every real response.

Do not stare at numbers all day.

Week one:

Make sure everything works.

Fix issues.

Thank people.

Share one or two strong moments.

Week two:

Ask for feedback.

Keep production moving.

Record or prepare the next episode.

Week three:

Share clips or quotes.

Reach out to possible guests or partners.

Watch what people respond to.

Week four:

Review lightly.

Adjust the next few episodes.

Keep going.

That is enough.

You do not need a parade.

You need a working door and a reason for people to walk through it.

## Closing Thought

Launch without making it weird.

That does not mean pretending it does not matter.

It means keeping it in perspective.

You made a thing.

Good.

Now help people find it.

Tell them who it is for.

Give them a reason to care.

Make the link easy.

Ask for one clear action.

Learn from what happens.

Then make the next episode.

Do not turn launch day into a final exam for your worth as a creator.

It is not.

It is a door opening.

Open it.

Let people in.

Then keep the show worth coming back to.

# Chapter 19: Hobby, Side Hustle, Business, or Legacy Project?

## Knowing what game you are playing before the show starts judging you.

Before we talk too much about money, sponsors, ads, affiliates, merch, memberships, live events, and all the other ways people can turn a show into a business, we need to slow down and ask a better question.

What is this show supposed to be for you?

Not what could it become someday if the internet blesses it with attention.

Not what some podcast guru says every creator should want.

Not what your friend thinks would be "huge."

Not what the algorithm seems to reward this week before changing its mind like a raccoon in a grocery store.

What is this show supposed to be for you?

Because not every show is playing the same game.

Some shows are hobbies.

Some are side hustles.

Some are businesses.

Some are marketing tools.

Some are community projects.

Some are legacy projects.

Some are creative outlets.

Some are emotional survival kits with microphones.

Some are all of those things at different times, which is where it can get messy.

This chapter matters because a lot of creators make themselves miserable by judging the show by the wrong scoreboard.

A family story show does not need to become a six-figure business to matter.

A business development show may not need a million downloads if it brings in three great clients.

A local community show may not need national attention if it becomes trusted in one town.

An audio fiction show may not need local sponsors if it is building a fan base.

A hobby show may not need revenue at all.

A side hustle probably does.

A legacy project might be worth doing even if only twelve people ever hear it, because those twelve people are the right twelve people.

The problem starts when we confuse the goal.

If you do not know what game you are playing, every scoreboard looks like a failure.

That is how a perfectly meaningful show starts feeling like it is not enough.

So before we chase money, we need to define success.

And no, "get huge" is not a definition.

That is a lottery ticket wearing a microphone.

## The Show Should Not Boss You Around

A show can become strangely demanding.

At first, it is just an idea.

A fun idea.

A little spark.

Something you talk about in the car or in the shower or while pretending to listen during a meeting that should have been an email.

Then you start working on it.

Now it wants a name.

Now it wants artwork.

Now it wants a format.

Now it wants a microphone.

Now it wants a website.

Now it wants clips.

Now it wants a newsletter.

Now it wants a launch plan.

Now it wants sponsors.

Now it wants you to understand analytics.

Now it wants you to post on platforms whose entire business model seems to be making adults feel like they are late to a party they did not want to attend.

At some point, the show starts acting like it owns you.

It does not.

You are making the show.

The show should serve a purpose in your life, your work, your creativity, or your community.

That purpose can be ambitious.

It can be simple.

It can be personal.

It can be commercial.

It can change.

But you need to name it.

Because an unnamed purpose becomes pressure.

And pressure without clarity turns into resentment.

## The Hobby Show

Let's start with the hobby show.

A hobby show is made because you like making it.

That is enough.

I know we live in a world where everything enjoyable is immediately dragged into the alley and asked how it plans to monetize. You like baking? Start a baking channel. You like fishing? Build a brand. You like old movies? Launch a Patreon. You like gardening? Create a course. You like taking walks? Somehow there is probably a funnel for that now.

Not everything has to become a business.

Some things are allowed to be enjoyed.

A hobby show can still be good.

A hobby show can still be consistent.

A hobby show can still have listeners.

A hobby show can still matter.

It just does not have to justify itself financially right away.

Maybe you and a friend talk about movies because you have been arguing about movies for thirty years anyway.

Maybe you record stories from your life because you like telling them.

Maybe you interview musicians in your town because you love the scene.

Maybe you make a show about old radio dramas because the subject makes you happy.

Maybe you recap baseball history because you need something in your life that is not an invoice, a password reset, or someone asking what is for dinner.

That is allowed.

## The Hobby Show Scoreboard

A hobby show should not be judged primarily by money.

Judge it by better questions.

Do I enjoy making it?

Am I getting better?

Do I feel more creative?

Is it connecting me to people I like?

Is it giving me a reason to learn?

Is it adding something good to my life?

Would I still make it if it never became a business?

That last question matters.

If the answer is yes, it may be a hobby show.

And that is not an insult.

Patti Smith — who built one of punk's most uncompromising careers — once said: "Don't make compromises, don't worry about making a bunch of money or being successful. Be concerned about doing good work."

She was not saying money is evil.

She was saying the work comes first.

The work has to be good enough, honest enough, and real enough that other things — including money — have somewhere to attach.

That applies here.

Some of the most honest creative work starts because somebody cares, not because somebody built a monetization plan in a spreadsheet.

A hobby show can become something else later.

But if you start it as a hobby, let it be a hobby.

Do not poison it by judging it like a startup.

## The Hobby Show Warning

A hobby show still needs boundaries.

Hobby does not mean chaos.

If you tell people it comes out every week and then disappear for three months, they may stop trusting it.

If you invite guests, you should respect their time.

If you publish publicly, you should still care about sound, clarity, and not wasting the listener's time.

But the pressure is different.

A hobby show can have a lighter schedule.

It can be seasonal.

It can be less polished.

It can prioritize joy.

It can skip monetization.

It can avoid social media platforms that make you want to throw your phone into a creek.

The danger is when a hobby show accidentally becomes a burden.

If that happens, shrink it.

Make it monthly.

Make it seasonal.

Record with a friend.

Stop doing video.

Stop making clips.

Stop turning the fun thing into a job you are not getting paid for.

If it is a hobby, protect the joy.

That is the whole point.

## The Side Hustle Show

A side hustle show is different.

A side hustle is supposed to make money eventually.

Maybe not immediately.

Maybe not a lot at first.

But the intention is different.

The show is still creative, but it also has a financial purpose.

That may mean sponsors.

Affiliates.

Paid memberships.

Digital products.

Courses.

Workshops.

Merch.

Live events.

Client leads.

Consulting.

Coaching.

Speaking.

Book sales.

A side hustle show lives between hobby and business.

It is not your full-time work, at least not yet.

But it needs to be treated with enough seriousness that money has somewhere to land.

This is where a lot of creators get confused.

They say they want the show to make money, but they build it like a hobby.

No sponsor page.

No email list.

No clear audience.

No offer.

No call to action.

No consistency.

No way for anyone to pay, hire, buy, book, sponsor, or support.

Then they wonder why the show is not making money.

That is not mysterious.

That is like opening a lemonade stand and forgetting the lemonade.

## The Side Hustle Scoreboard

A side hustle show should be judged by both creative and financial signals.

Do I enjoy the work enough to keep going?

Is the audience clear?

Is the show growing trust?

Are people joining the email list?

Are people clicking affiliate links?

Are sponsors interested?

Are listeners asking for help?

Are the right people finding me?

Is the show creating opportunities?

Is the money model clear?

Am I spending more than makes sense?

Do I have a path from listener to customer, supporter, sponsor, or buyer?

A side hustle does not have to make money on day one.

But it should be moving toward a model.

If there is no model, it may still be a hobby.

That is fine.

Just do not lie to yourself.

## The Side Hustle Warning

The danger of a side hustle is that it can become all hustle and no show.

You start with a creative idea, and before long, everything is a funnel.

Every episode is an offer.

Every guest is a lead.

Every listener is a target.

Every post is an angle.

That can make the show feel gross.

People can smell it.

The audience does not mind you making money.

Most reasonable adults understand that things cost money.

They mind feeling like they are being handled.

So with a side hustle show, lead with value.

Make the show worth listening to.

Make the audience trust you.

Make the offer clear but not desperate.

Money follows trust better than it follows pressure.

## The Business Show

A business show is built to support a business.

This is not always the same thing as the show being the business.

That distinction matters.

For example, a law firm might create a show to explain common legal questions. The show itself may not make money from ads. It brings trust and clients.

A real estate professional might create a local market show. The show builds authority, relationships, and leads.

A consultant might create a show about leadership, AI, marketing, finance, health, or operations. The show demonstrates expertise and brings in clients.

A media company might create a network of shows and sell sponsorships, production, events, or advertising around them.

A business show may be judged less by downloads and more by business outcomes.

Did someone book a call?

Did a sponsor renew?

Did the show create a partnership?

Did it shorten the sales cycle?

Did it position the host as the person who understands the problem?

Did it make the business easier to trust?

That is a different scoreboard.

## The Business Show Scoreboard

A business show should measure:

Qualified leads.

Client conversations.

Sponsor interest.

Partnerships.

Email signups.

Website visits.

Sales calls.

Customer education.

Trust.

Search visibility.

Referral traffic.

Authority.

Speaking opportunities.

Media opportunities.

Audience fit.

Downloads and views still matter, but they may not be the main thing.

A business show with 300 perfect listeners may be more valuable than a general entertainment show with 10,000 casual ones.

If the right person listens and hires you, the show worked.

Do not let vanity metrics insult a useful business tool.

## The Business Show Warning

The danger of a business show is boredom.

A lot of business content sounds like it was created in a conference room where joy was not allowed past security.

Do not do that.

Business people are still people.

They like stories.

They like humor.

They like clear language.

They like examples.

They like honesty.

They like someone saying the thing plainly.

A business show should not be a brochure with theme music.

It should be useful.

If your audience has a problem, help them understand it.

If they are making a mistake, show them.

If there is a better way, explain it.

If you have a story, tell it.

If you have an opinion, say it.

The business goal does not excuse boring.

In fact, the business goal makes clarity and story more important.

## The Authority Show

This overlaps with the business show, but it deserves its own lane.

An authority show is built to make the host known for something.

It may lead to business, but its first job is positioning.

This is the show for the person who wants to be associated with a topic, industry, movement, mission, or point of view.

Maybe you are the person who explains AI to small-town business owners.

Maybe you are the person who interviews local creators.

Maybe you are the person who talks about sports media, true crime ethics, podcasting for older creators, nonprofit leadership, second careers, or forgotten local history.

Authority is not the same as arrogance.

Authority means the audience starts associating you with a useful point of view.

That can be powerful.

## The Authority Scoreboard

An authority show should measure:

Are people quoting the ideas?

Are guests saying yes?

Are other shows inviting you on?

Are people asking for your opinion?

Are you ranking for relevant topics?

Are you being introduced as the person who knows this subject?

Are opportunities appearing because of the show?

Are you building a body of work?

Authority grows through consistency.

Not one viral post.

A body of work.

A library.

A trail.

Episode by episode, you are teaching people what you are about.

## The Legacy Project

Now let's talk about something that may be more important than money.

A legacy project.

A legacy project is created because something needs to be preserved, said, recorded, or passed on.

Family stories.

Community history.

Veteran stories.

Church history.

Business origin stories.

Local music scenes.

Old neighborhoods.

Personal recovery.

Letters to children or grandchildren.

Conversations with parents.

Stories from people who will not be here forever.

Lessons from a life.

This may be one of the most meaningful reasons to make a show.

And it may not care one bit about downloads.

A legacy project might be successful if twenty family members hear it.

Or if one grandson hears his grandfather's voice years from now.

Or if a town has a record of people and places that would have been forgotten.

Or if a retired teacher, coach, nurse, mechanic, pastor, business owner, musician, or parent gets to tell the stories that never made it into the official record.

That matters.

Do not let the internet's obsession with scale make you think small audiences cannot carry big meaning.

Manu Ginobili — who won four championships with the Spurs and could have spent his whole career building a brand around his legacy — put it this way: "If you live your life thinking about your legacy or what you're going to leave, you add another concern. Just live your life every single day, do the best you can — and that's more of my motto than leaving a legacy."

This is worth sitting with.

A legacy project matters because the work matters.

Not because you are engineering a monument.

If you start a family history show because you want your grandchildren to know who their great-grandparents were, that is a legacy project.

If you start recording because you want to preserve your community before it changes, that is a legacy project.

If you start because you have stories that deserve to exist somewhere other than inside your own head, that is a legacy project.

Start because the thing deserves to exist.

The legacy takes care of itself.

## The Legacy Project Scoreboard

A legacy project should measure:

Did we record the story?

Did we preserve the voice?

Did we capture details that would have disappeared?

Did the right people receive it?

Did it honor the subject?

Did it create a record?

Did it help someone feel seen?

Did it give the family or community something to keep?

That is a different kind of success.

It may never trend.

It may never get sponsors.

It may never need a social strategy.

But it may matter more than half the things online with better numbers.

## The Legacy Project Warning

The danger of a legacy project is waiting too long.

This is the hard part.

People think they have time.

We always think we have time.

I will record Dad's stories later.

I will interview Grandma next month.

I will ask about the old business someday.

I will get the family history down when things slow down.

Things do not slow down.

People get sick.

Memories fade.

Voices disappear.

Photos lose names.

Places close.

Stories get smaller every time someone who remembers them is gone.

If the show is a legacy project, start.

It does not have to be perfect.

It has to exist.

A bad recording of someone you love telling the truth is worth more than a perfect recording you never made.

## The Community Project

A community project is built to serve a group.

It may be local.

It may be niche.

It may be a professional community, fan community, neighborhood, school, church, nonprofit, creative scene, sports community, or recovery community.

The goal is connection.

A community show gives people a place to hear themselves reflected.

It shares stories.

It celebrates people.

It asks questions.

It creates a record.

It can also create partnerships, sponsors, events, and civic value.

But the heart is service.

A community show should ask:

Who is being served?

Who is being included?

Who is usually ignored?

What stories are missing?

What does this community need to understand about itself?

That is a powerful reason to make a show.

## The Community Scoreboard

A community project should measure:

Are people participating?

Are they submitting stories?

Are they sharing episodes?

Are local groups connecting?

Are guests saying yes?

Are people learning about each other?

Are events growing from the show?

Are sponsors or partners aligned with the community?

Is the show making the community feel more visible?

That is success.

Not just downloads.

A local show with comments, emails, calls, stories, and people stopping you at events may be healthier than a show with passive plays and no relationship.

## The Creative Outlet

Sometimes the show exists because the creator needs a place to make something.

That is real.

Maybe your job is practical, and you need something creative.

Maybe your kids are grown, and you are trying to rediscover who you are.

Maybe you spent years taking care of everyone else and forgot what it felt like to make something for yourself.

Maybe you have a competitive spark that never went away, and you need somewhere to put it that is not yelling at televised sports.

Maybe you are sober now and creativity gives your brain something better to build.

Maybe you spent years thinking about making audio fiction, comedy, music conversations, sports talk, interviews, or family stories, and now you finally have the tools.

A creative outlet matters.

It may not start as money.

It may start as oxygen.

That is not small.

## The Creative Outlet Scoreboard

A creative outlet should measure:

Am I making things again?

Am I learning?

Am I proud of the work?

Am I more myself because this exists?

Is the show helping me think?

Is it giving me a healthy place to compete?

Is it connecting me to people?

Is it making my life bigger, not smaller?

If yes, the show is working.

Even if the numbers are not flashy.

Sometimes the first job of a show is to wake something up in the person making it.

That is worth respecting.

## The Mission Show

A mission show is created to move an idea forward.

It may be about a cause, faith, advocacy, education, recovery, health, justice, reform, local change, or awareness.

The goal is not only audience.

The goal is impact.

A mission show needs clarity because mission-driven creators can sometimes assume the importance is obvious.

It may be obvious to you.

It is not always obvious to a new listener.

You still need story.

You still need structure.

You still need specific audience.

You still need to make the show listenable.

Being right does not automatically make you interesting.

Sorry.

But it is true.

A mission show has to carry the mission in a way people can actually receive.

## The Mission Scoreboard

A mission show should measure:

Are people learning?

Are people taking action?

Are the right conversations happening?

Are partners joining?

Are stories being heard?

Are resources being shared?

Are people changing behavior?

Are decision-makers listening?

Are affected people represented well?

Are we building trust?

Those are impact measures.

Downloads matter, but they may not tell the whole story.

## Mixed Motives Are Normal

Here is the truth.

Most shows are not only one thing.

You might want creative expression and money.

You might want community and sponsors.

You might want legacy and a book.

You might want a hobby that maybe becomes a side hustle.

You might want a business show that is also deeply personal.

That is normal.

People are layered.

Motives are layered.

The point is not to purify your reason until it sounds noble enough for a grant application.

The point is to know the primary reason.

What is the main job of the show right now?

Right now matters.

Not forever.

A show can change phases.

A hobby can become a side hustle.

A side hustle can become a business.

A business show can become a legacy body of work.

A community show can attract sponsors.

A creative outlet can become a career.

But if you try to make the first version satisfy every possible future version, you will overbuild it.

Pick the primary job for now.

Then build around that.

## The Wrong Scoreboard Problem

Let's name the problem clearly.

A show gets hurt when it is judged by the wrong scoreboard.

A hobby show judged by revenue will feel like a failure.

A business show judged only by downloads may ignore the clients it brings.

A legacy project judged by social shares will feel invisible, even if it deeply matters to the family.

A community show judged by national growth may miss its local impact.

A side hustle judged like a hobby may never build a path to money.

A mission show judged only by entertainment may forget impact.

This is why goal-setting matters before monetization.

Money is one possible measure.

It is not the only measure.

Even when money matters, it may not be the first measure.

Trust may come first.

Clarity may come first.

Audience fit may come first.

Consistency may come first.

Proof may come first.

If you pick the wrong scoreboard, you will make the wrong decisions.

## The Cost Question

Every show has a cost.

Money, yes.

But also time, attention, energy, family patience, creative focus, opportunity cost, and mental space.

Be honest about the cost.

A hobby show should not wreck your family schedule.

A side hustle should have a path toward paying for itself.

A business show should justify its time through real business value.

A legacy project may be worth the time even if there is no money.

A mission show may need partners so the creator does not burn out.

A creative outlet should give back energy somewhere, even if it takes work.

Ask:

What will this show cost me?

What do I hope it gives back?

Is that trade fair?

If the trade is not fair, change the show.

Shorter.

Seasonal.

Simpler.

Less video.

Fewer platforms.

More help.

Clearer monetization.

Different format.

The show does not get to consume your life just because it is creative.

Creative work still needs boundaries.

## The Money Question

Now we can ask about money more honestly.

Does this show need to make money?

If yes, how soon?

How much?

From whom?

Through what model?

Sponsors?

Services?

Affiliates?

Products?

Membership?

Events?

Donations?

Clients?

Book sales?

Courses?

Grants?

Underwriting?

If the show does not need to make money, does it still need a budget?

Hosting costs money.

Gear costs money.

Software costs money.

Time costs something, even if nobody sends an invoice.

You do not need to monetize everything, but you do need to know what the show can afford.

A hobby show can have a small fun budget.

A legacy project may need a one-time production budget.

A business show may be funded by the business.

A community show may need sponsors or grants.

A side hustle needs a revenue path.

Money is not evil.

Confusion around money is the problem.

## The Audience Promise Changes by Goal

Your goal affects the promise.

A hobby show might promise fun, personality, and consistency.

A side hustle show might promise value and eventually offer paid help.

A business show might promise expertise and trust.

A legacy project might promise preservation.

A community show might promise representation and connection.

A mission show might promise awareness and action.

A creative outlet might promise honesty and exploration.

The audience should not have to guess.

They do not need a full business plan.

But they should understand the relationship.

If the show is a business show, it is okay to say who you help and how.

If the show is a community project, invite participation.

If the show is a legacy project, explain the preservation mission.

If the show is a creative outlet, let the audience know they are along for the ride.

Clarity builds trust.

## Examples of the Same Topic With Different Goals

Let's take the same topic: AI for older creators.

As a hobby show:

Two friends try AI tools each week and laugh through what works and what absolutely does not.

Success: fun, learning, community, consistency.

As a side hustle:

A creator reviews AI tools and offers templates, guides, affiliate links, and workshops.

Success: email signups, affiliate clicks, product sales.

As a business show:

An agency owner teaches small businesses how to use AI without sounding fake, leading to consulting clients.

Success: leads, calls, clients, authority.

As a legacy project:

A retired educator records conversations with older creators learning new tools so their stories are not lost.

Success: preserved stories, family/community value.

As a mission show:

A nonprofit teaches older adults how to use AI safely so they are not left behind.

Success: education, access, reduced fear, partnerships.

Same topic.

Different goals.

Different scoreboard.

Different show design.

That is why this chapter matters.

## Another Example: Local History

Same topic: local history.

Hobby:

You and a friend talk about old restaurants, shops, school memories, and local legends.

Business:

A local media company builds a show that attracts sponsors from banks, museums, restaurants, real estate groups, and tourism partners.

Community:

Residents submit stories and photos, and the show becomes a shared archive.

Legacy:

You interview elders before their stories disappear.

Mission:

The show highlights neighborhoods and voices left out of the official record.

Same topic.

Different purpose.

Different structure.

Different money model.

Different success.

If you know the purpose, the decisions get easier.

## The Personal Honesty Part

This is where you need to be honest with yourself.

Do you actually want a business?

Or do you want the feeling of being taken seriously?

Do you want sponsors?

Or do you want proof that the show matters?

Do you want a large audience?

Or do you want the right people to respect the work?

Do you want to make money?

Or do you want permission to spend time on something creative?

Do you want a legacy project?

Or are you avoiding the vulnerability of calling it a business?

There are no wrong answers.

There are dishonest answers.

And dishonest answers make bad shows.

If you want money, say you want money.

If you want joy, say you want joy.

If you want clients, say you want clients.

If you want to preserve your father's stories, say that.

If you want to be known for something, say that.

If you want to prove to yourself you can still make something, say that.

The show can handle the truth.

It is the pretending that makes everything weird.

## The Goal Can Change

Give yourself permission to change the goal later.

A show may start as a hobby and become a side hustle.

That is fine.

A business show may become a mission.

A creative outlet may become a book.

A local show may become an event series.

A family history project may become a public archive.

A side hustle may need to become a hobby again because life changes.

That is allowed.

But when the goal changes, update the show.

Do not keep using the old structure for the new purpose.

If it becomes a business, build the business pieces.

If it becomes a hobby, release some pressure.

If it becomes a legacy project, focus on preservation.

If it becomes a community project, invite participation.

If it becomes a mission show, build partners and resources.

A show can grow.

Just do not let it drift without naming the change.

## The One-Sentence Goal

Before moving into monetization, write one sentence.

The main job of this show is to:

______________________________________________

That sentence might be:

The main job of this show is to help me reconnect with creativity and make something every week.

The main job of this show is to build trust with small business owners who may eventually hire us.

The main job of this show is to preserve family stories before they disappear.

The main job of this show is to become a side hustle through sponsors, affiliate links, and workshops.

The main job of this show is to serve our local community by telling stories that are not being covered elsewhere.

The main job of this show is to build authority around AI for people over fifty.

That sentence is a compass.

Use it.

When decisions get confusing, come back to it.

Should we add video?

Depends on the goal.

Should we sell sponsors?

Depends on the goal.

Should we post on TikTok?

Depends on the goal.

Should we spend money on editing?

Depends on the goal.

Should we make this weekly?

Depends on the goal.

Your goal does not answer everything automatically, but it gives you a place to start.

## Closing Thought

Before you ask how the show makes money, ask what the show is for.

Hobby.

Side hustle.

Business.

Authority.

Legacy.

Community.

Mission.

Creative outlet.

Some mix of those.

Name it.

Not because you have to lock it forever.

Because you need the right scoreboard.

The wrong scoreboard will make you feel like you are failing when you are actually doing exactly what the show was meant to do.

A legacy project does not need to go viral.

A business show does not need to entertain everybody.

A hobby show does not need a funnel.

A community show does not need national fame.

A side hustle does need a revenue path.

A mission show does need impact.

A creative outlet does need to keep the creator alive in some way.

Know the game.

Then play that game.

Not somebody else's.

Yours.

# Chapter 20: Don't Make Future You Hire a Lawyer

## Music, clips, guests, sponsors, names, claims, AI, and other ways to avoid stepping on a rake.

Let me say this right at the top.

I am not your lawyer.

This chapter is not legal advice.

This chapter is the grown-up, common-sense, "please do not make future you spend money fixing something current you could have avoided" chapter.

And yes, that is a real category.

If your show gets big, if you start making money, if you are working with sponsors, if you are using other people's music, if you are talking about crimes, if you are giving serious advice, if you are building a business around the show, or if you just have that little feeling in your stomach that says, "Can I do this?" then ask an actual lawyer.

Not a Facebook group.

Not a guy at lunch who once had a cousin with a trademark.

Not an AI chatbot.

An actual lawyer.

But most early mistakes are not exotic legal mysteries.

They are basic avoidable things.

Using music you do not own.

Using clips you do not have permission to use.

Naming your show too close to someone else's.

Having guests on with no written permission.

Making claims you cannot support.

Running sponsor reads without disclosure.

Talking about real people carelessly.

Using AI-generated voices or images in misleading ways.

Promising things in sponsor emails that you cannot deliver.

This chapter is not here to scare you.

It is here to keep you from stepping on rakes.

Because rakes are everywhere.

And sometimes the rake has an invoice attached.

## The "It's Fine" Voice Is Not a Legal Strategy

Most bad decisions begin with a voice that says:

"It's probably fine."

Sometimes it is fine.

Sometimes it is not.

The problem is that "probably fine" gets expensive when you are wrong.

You use thirty seconds of a popular song because "everybody does it."

You use a movie clip because "it's fair use."

You name the show after a phrase from a TV show because "it's just a tribute."

You read a sponsor script and forget to disclose the relationship because "the audience will know."

You accuse someone of something because "I heard it from a reliable guy."

You use an AI clone voice because "it's obviously parody."

Maybe nothing happens.

Or maybe something happens.

A takedown.

A demonetized video.

A sponsor problem.

A cease-and-desist letter.

A guest complaint.

A platform strike.

A lawsuit.

A public trust problem.

The fact that other people got away with something does not mean you should build your show on it.

Other people speed too.

That does not make the ticket imaginary.

## Music: No, You Cannot Just Use That Song

This is probably the biggest one.

Music feels emotional.

Music sets tone.

Music makes things feel like a show.

Music can make your intro sound professional, your trailer feel bigger, your scene feel sad, your sports montage feel epic, and your outro feel like you have your life together.

But music has rights.

Generally, someone owns the composition.

Someone may own the sound recording.

There may be multiple people, publishers, labels, performers, and rights holders involved.

That song you love from 1987?

You probably cannot just use it because it "fits the vibe."

I know.

It is annoying.

It would be great if every show could open with the perfect old song and nobody cared.

That is not the world.

If you use copyrighted music without permission, you may get flagged, muted, demonetized, blocked, taken down, or worse.

And if you are building a serious show, especially one with sponsors or a business around it, do not start with stolen music vibes.

That is not a brand identity.

That is a future problem with a beat.

## Use Music You Have the Right to Use

You have options.

Use royalty-free music from reputable libraries.

Use music with a license that clearly allows your use.

Commission original music.

Use music you created.

Use music from a local artist with a written agreement.

Use platform-provided music only according to that platform's rules.

Read the license.

I know.

Nobody wants to read the license.

Read it anyway.

Does it allow podcast use?

Commercial use?

YouTube use?

Advertising?

Paid promotion?

Broadcast?

Social clips?

Forever?

Worldwide?

Can you edit it?

Do you need attribution?

Can you keep using it if you stop subscribing?

These details matter.

Do not assume “royalty-free” means “do whatever you want until the sun burns out.”

It does not always mean that.

## Clips: Fair Use Is Not a Magic Spell

Now let’s talk about clips.

Movie clips.

TV clips.

Sports clips.

News clips.

Music videos.

TikToks.

YouTube videos.

Press conference footage.

Old commercials.

Whatever.

Creators love saying “fair use.”

It is one of those phrases people say with way more confidence than they should.

Fair use is real.

It is also not a magic spell.

You do not just say “fair use” three times and become legally protected like a wizard with a ring light.

Fair use depends on multiple factors, including the purpose and character of the use, the nature of the copyrighted work, the amount used, and the effect on the market for the original.

That means context matters.

Commentary, criticism, education, news reporting, and parody may have stronger arguments than simply using a clip because it looks cool.

But it is still a legal analysis, not a vibe.

Platforms may take content down even if you believe you have a fair use argument.

Then you have to decide whether to fight it.

That takes time.

And possibly money.

So be smart.

If you do not need the clip, do not use the clip.

If you use the clip, use only what you need.

Add real commentary or transformation.

Do not just replay someone else's work.

And if the show depends heavily on copyrighted clips, talk to someone who understands this before building the whole thing.

## Sports Clips Are Especially Tricky

Sports content is tempting.

Highlights.

Game footage.

Broadcast clips.

Press conferences.

Radio calls.

Crowd shots.

The problem is that sports rights are often tightly controlled.

Leagues, networks, schools, conferences, teams, and platforms may all have rules.

Just because a clip is online does not mean you can use it.

Just because someone else posted it does not mean you can use it.

Just because you are talking about it does not automatically make it safe.

If you are making a sports show, you can still be great without relying on copyrighted footage.

Use commentary.

Use analysis.

Use stills you have rights to.

Use graphics.

Use your own footage where permitted.

Use licensed clips if available.

Use public press conference material according to the rules.

But do not build your show around ripping game footage and hoping nobody notices.

Somebody may notice.

And they may have more lawyers than you.

## Guest Releases: Get Permission in Writing

If someone is appearing on your show, get permission in writing.

This does not have to be complicated, especially for a simple show.

But you want a written record that they agreed to be recorded and that you can use, edit, publish, promote, and distribute the episode.

An email can help.

A formal release is better for serious productions.

For bigger projects, documentaries, audio fiction, paid performances, sensitive topics, minors, or commercial use, get a real release drafted or reviewed by a lawyer.

Do not rely on "they knew we were recording."

Maybe they did.

Maybe they later remember it differently.

A guest release protects the show, the guest, and the relationship.

It also makes you look professional.

And if you are recording video, using clips, making promotional materials, or selling sponsorship around the episode, the permission matters even more.

## Guest Release Basics

A basic guest release should answer:

Who is being recorded?

What show or project is it for?

What date?

Can the recording be edited?

Can it be published in audio and video?

Can clips be used for promotion?

Can their name, likeness, voice, and bio be used?

Can the episode be distributed on podcast apps, YouTube, websites, social media, newsletters, and future platforms?

Are they being paid or appearing voluntarily?

Who owns the final recording?

Can the creator monetize the episode?

Again, I am not giving you legal language here.

I am telling you what issues need to be handled.

Use a proper release if the show is serious.

Future you will appreciate it.

Future you is already tired.

## Be Careful With Minors

If minors are involved, slow down.

Do not casually record kids and publish them because it seems cute.

Get parental permission.

Understand school, sports, event, and organizational rules.

Be careful with identifying details.

Be careful with sensitive topics.

Be especially careful with true crime, family issues, health, trauma, or anything that could follow a kid online.

The internet does not forget in the way we wish it would.

If a child is part of the show, protect them first.

The episode can wait.

## Sponsors and Disclosures

If a sponsor pays you, gives you free products, gives you discounts, gives you travel, gives you anything of value, or there is another material relationship, disclose it clearly.

Do not make people guess.

Do not hide it in tiny text.

Do not call everything a "partner" and hope that covers it.

Say what it is.

"This episode is sponsored by..."

"We received this product for free..."

"This link is an affiliate link..."

"Thanks to [Sponsor] for supporting the show..."

Clear is better than cute.

The FTC's guidance is straightforward on this point: if there is a financial, employment, personal, family, or other material relationship with a brand, it should be disclosed clearly.

That includes free or discounted products if you mention them.

This is not just about staying out of trouble.

It is about trust.

Your audience will forgive a sponsor.

They may not forgive feeling tricked.

## YouTube and Platform Disclosures

If you publish on YouTube and your content includes paid product placement, sponsorship, endorsement, or another commercial relationship, YouTube has disclosure tools and policies around that.

Use them.

But do not assume a platform checkbox is the whole job.

You may still need to disclose clearly in the video, audio, description, or wherever the endorsement appears.

The platform tool can help.

It does not replace your responsibility to be clear with the audience.

If the ad is in the content, the disclosure should be hard to miss.

Not hidden like a secret level in an old video game.

## Sponsor Agreements

When money is involved, put the agreement in writing.

Please.

Even if it is simple.

Especially if it is simple.

A sponsor agreement should include:

Sponsor name.

Show name.

Dates.

Number of episodes.

Placement type.

Ad length.

Deliverables.

Links.

Social posts or clips if included.

Logo use.

Payment amount.

Payment due date.

What happens if an episode is delayed.

What happens if the sponsor cancels.

What happens if the show cancels.

Reporting expectations.

Any exclusivity.

Approval process.

Disclosure language.

Who owns what.

You do not need a fifty-page contract for a small local sponsor.

But you need a written agreement.

Emails can help.

A signed agreement is better.

The goal is not to be difficult.

The goal is to avoid the awkward conversation later when everybody remembers the deal differently.

## Names and Trademarks

Naming a show is fun until you realize someone else already has a similar name.

Do a search before you get attached.

Search podcast apps.

Search YouTube.

Search Google.

Search social media.

Search domain names.

Search the USPTO trademark database if you are in the United States and building something serious.

The issue is not only whether the names are identical.

Trademark confusion can involve names that sound similar, look similar, mean similar things, or create a similar commercial impression, especially if the goods or services are related.

That is the part people miss.

"But mine has a Z."

That may not save you.

"But theirs is two words and mine is one word."

Maybe not.

"But I spelled it worse."

Congratulations, still maybe a problem.

If you are planning to build a brand, sell merch, get sponsors, create a network, or write a book under the name, check early.

Changing later is annoying.

Changing after a cease-and-desist is more annoying.

## True Crime and Real Accusations

If you do true crime, investigations, local scandal, politics, business disputes, or anything involving real people and allegations, be careful.

This is not the lane for sloppy talk.

Do not accuse people casually.

Do not present rumors as facts.

Do not imply guilt without evidence.

Do not identify private people unnecessarily.

Do not treat victims as story props.

Do not use tragedy as seasoning.

Do not forget families may be listening.

True crime can be powerful when handled with care.

It can also be gross.

And legally risky.

If you are discussing active cases, unsolved crimes, named suspects, private individuals, or sensitive allegations, verify.

Use primary documents where possible.

Attribute clearly.

Say what is known.

Say what is alleged.

Say what is opinion.

Do not overstate.

If you do not know, say you do not know.

The audience can handle uncertainty.

They cannot trust carelessness.

## Defamation, Opinions, and Being Too Casual

People sometimes think, “It is just my opinion,” protects everything.

It does not.

Opinions are safer when they are clearly opinions based on disclosed facts.

But if you state or imply false facts that harm someone's reputation, you may create legal risk.

Again, lawyer territory if you are doing serious reporting or accusations.

Common sense helps.

Say:

"In my opinion..."

"The documents show..."

"According to the complaint..."

"The family says..."

"The police reported..."

"We have not independently verified..."

"What we know is..."

"What remains unclear is..."

Do not say:

"He definitely did it," unless that has actually been legally established and you are accurately reporting it.

Do not turn speculation into certainty because certainty sounds better in a clip.

A good show can be compelling without being reckless.

## Medical, Financial, and Legal Advice

If your show touches medical, financial, legal, mental health, taxes, investments, health products, supplements, or other high-stakes topics, be careful.

This does not mean you cannot talk about them.

It means you should know what you are doing.

Do not present general discussion as personalized professional advice.

Use disclaimers where appropriate.

Encourage people to talk to qualified professionals.

Do not make claims you cannot support.

Do not let sponsors pressure you into claims.

Do not say a product treats, cures, prevents, or fixes something unless that claim is properly supported and legally allowed.

The more serious the consequence, the more careful the show needs to be.

A bad movie take is one thing.

Bad medical advice is another.

## AI Voices, Images, and Deepfakes

AI brings new ways to step on rakes.

Do not clone someone's voice without permission.

Do not use someone's face or likeness misleadingly.

Do not create fake endorsements.

Do not make it look like a guest said something they did not say.

Do not create synthetic "evidence" for a real story.

Do not use AI images in a way that confuses reality when reality matters.

If you use AI-generated material, be honest when honesty matters.

Not every AI-assisted graphic needs a courtroom announcement.

But if the audience could reasonably be misled, disclose.

If the show depends on trust, do not play cute games with reality.

The technology may be new.

The principle is old:

Do not trick people.

## Keep Records

Save things.

Contracts.

Guest releases.

Sponsor emails.

Music licenses.

Artwork licenses.

Stock photo licenses.

AI tool terms if relevant.

Receipts.

Permissions.

Screenshots of agreements.

Approved ad copy.

Episode dates.

Sponsor reports.

If you use a song, save the license.

If a guest approves use, save the release.

If a sponsor approves copy, save the email.

If you commissioned artwork, save the agreement.

This is boring.

Boring is good.

Boring is how future you proves what happened.

A creator with organized records is in a better position than a creator saying, "I'm pretty sure we talked about that."

Pretty sure is not a filing system.

## When to Ask a Lawyer

Ask a lawyer when:

The show is becoming a business.

You are taking sponsor money regularly.

You are using contracts.

You are hiring talent, editors, writers, or producers.

You are using copyrighted material in a significant way.

You are doing true crime or investigative work.

You are making claims about real people or businesses.

You are dealing with minors.

You are creating a network.

You are licensing content.

You are selling products, memberships, courses, or events.

You are unsure and the stakes are high.

Legal help costs money.

So does legal trouble.

Sometimes paying a lawyer for an hour early is cheaper than paying one for weeks later.

This is one of those grown-up things nobody wants to hear until they need it.

## The Common-Sense Legal Checklist

Before publishing, ask:

Do I have the right to use the music?

Do I have the right to use the clips/images?

Do I have guest permission?

Are sponsor relationships disclosed?

Are affiliate links disclosed?

Are claims supported?

Am I careful with real people and accusations?

Am I using AI in a way that could mislead?

Do I have written agreements where money or permission matters?

Have I saved the records?

Do I need legal advice?

If this checklist makes you nervous, good.

Not paralyzed.

Just awake.

Awake is useful.

## Closing Thought

This chapter is not here to scare you out of making a show.

Make the show.

Please.

But make it like someone who understands that the internet is not a magical law-free playground just because other people act like it is.

Use music you have rights to.

Be careful with clips.

Get guest permission.

Disclose sponsors.

Check names.

Support claims.

Respect real people.

Do not use AI to trick anybody.

Put agreements in writing.

Save the records.

And when the stakes are high, ask a lawyer.

Future you has enough to do.

Do not make future you hire a lawyer because current you wanted to use a Bon Jovi song for the intro.

No offense to Bon Jovi.

That chorus probably did slap.

Still, get permission.

# Chapter 21: Money Comes After Trust

At some point, every creator thinks about money. That is normal. Money is not a dirty word. If you put time, equipment, hosting fees, editing, research, and part of your life into a show, it is fair to wonder if it can pay for itself.

But the first monetization question is not, “How do I get paid?” The first question is: have I built enough trust for money to make sense here?

Money comes after trust.

## Sponsor-Ready Comes Before Sponsor-Paid

Most new shows should not start by chasing sponsors. They should start by becoming sponsor-ready. A sponsor-ready show has a clear name, clear artwork, clear audience, reliable schedule, home base, strong episodes, and a professional way to include a sponsor.

A lot of people want sponsor money to prove the show is real. That is backward. Make the show real first.

## The Audience Is Not Inventory

Your audience is not a pile of ad slots. They are people who gave you time. Do not sell them out cheaply.

Trent Reznor of Nine Inch Nails put it plainly: "I'm just trying to figure out the right balance between making fans feel good and also maintaining some dignity for myself in the process."

That tension does not go away when money enters the picture.

In some ways it gets sharper.

Because now the question is not just whether the show is good. The question is whether the commercial pieces fit without making the whole thing feel like a transaction.

A good show can support a sponsor and still feel like itself.

A show that chases every dollar loses the thing people came for.

The balance is not perfect. You will make judgment calls. Some will feel right. Some you will second-guess at midnight.

But starting from "do no harm to the audience trust" is the right place to start.

The right sponsor can make sense. Random garbage because someone offered a few bucks can damage trust fast.

## Be Your Own First Sponsor

If you do not have sponsors yet, act like you do. Not by lying. By practicing.

Create a house ad for your own email list, website, YouTube channel, event, free guide, business, services, or another show in your network. Treat it like a real ad slot. Write it, record it, place it cleanly, make it sound intentional.

A house ad is not fake. It is practice. It also gives you a sample to show future sponsors.

## Free Can Be Smart, But Be Clear

Doing a free sponsorship can make sense if you want proof, a testimonial, a case study, or a community partnership. But do it on purpose. Call it a trial sponsorship, launch partner opportunity, community partnership, trade, or founding sponsor pilot.

Set a beginning and end. Define what they get. Ask for feedback, testimonial, or permission to use results.

Do not give away inventory forever because you are afraid to charge.

## Do Not Fake Trust

Do not pretend a brand paid when it did not. Do not recommend something you do not believe in. Do not hide free products, discounts, trade, or material relationships.

The better version of "fake it till you make it" is not pretending. It is rehearsing the professional version before the professional version arrives.

Be sponsor-ready before you are sponsor-paid.

## Money Models

Shows can make money through host-read sponsorships, dynamic/programmatic ads, affiliate links, listener support, memberships, premium episodes, merch, live events, courses, books, consulting, services, lead generation, network deals, and more.

You do not need all of them. Pick the model that fits the show. A local sports show may work with local sponsors and live events. A business show may create leads. Audio fiction may use memberships, bonus content, merch, or crowdfunding. A how-to show may use affiliates or courses.

The money model should fit the show, not the other way around.

## Simple Sponsor Packages

Do not make sponsor packages so complicated that even you need a decoder ring.

Start with simple.

**Episode Sponsor**

One episode. One host-read mention. Link in show notes. Optional logo if video.

**Monthly Sponsor**

Four episodes. Host-read mention in each. Website link. Social mention or clip tag. Monthly recap.

**Founding Sponsor**

Limited early partner package for the first season or first ten episodes. Includes recognition as an early supporter and a lower launch rate.

**Segment Sponsor**

A recurring piece of the show is "brought to you by" a sponsor. Works best when the segment and sponsor naturally fit.

**Community Partner**

For nonprofits, events, or local partners. May be paid, trade, or promotional depending on the agreement.

That is enough.

You can get fancy later.

Simple sells better because people can understand it.

## Pricing Without Panic

Pricing is hard because it feels personal.

It is not.

You are pricing access, attention, association, production, trust, and deliverables.

Do not price only by downloads if the show is small but specific.

A local show with modest numbers can still be valuable to a local business.

A niche professional show can be valuable because the audience is hard to reach.

A sponsor may care about the host relationship more than raw impressions.

That said, do not invent numbers.

Do not promise what you cannot prove.

If your audience is small, sell the fit.

Sell the trust.

Sell the repeated presence.

Sell the community connection.

Sell the fact that the audience is not random.

You can say:

"We are early, so we are offering founding sponsor rates while we build the audience."

That is honest.

Better than pretending you are bigger than you are.

## Sponsor Reporting

If someone sponsors the show, send a recap.

It does not need to be a corporate report with seventeen charts and a photo of two people shaking hands.

Keep it simple.

Episodes included.

Dates published.

Downloads or views available.

Clip performance.

Social posts.

Website links.

Audience comments if relevant.

Screenshots.

Next steps.

This makes you look professional.

It also helps the sponsor understand what they bought.

If the numbers are small, focus on consistency, presentation, audience fit, and proof that the placements happened.

Sponsors appreciate not having to chase you.

Be the person who sends the recap.

That alone puts you ahead of a lot of people.

## Affiliates Without Selling Your Soul

Affiliate links can be useful if they genuinely fit the show.

If you recommend microphones, hosting platforms, books, software, AI tools, courses, or products your audience actually needs, affiliate links can make sense.

But do not turn the show into a flea market.

The audience should never feel like every recommendation is for sale.

Use affiliate links with trust.

Disclose them.

Keep a resource page.

Recommend what you would recommend even if the payout were smaller.

If you would not tell a friend to use it, do not tell your audience.

That is a clean rule.

## Live Events and Money

Live events can be powerful, especially for local, niche, or personality-driven shows.

A live recording.

A small meetup.

A panel.

A workshop.

A screening.

A storytelling night.

A sponsor-backed community event.

These can create revenue and deepen audience loyalty.

But live events are work.

Venue.

Sound.

Tickets.

Promotion.

Staff.

Insurance.

Sponsors.

Run of show.

Weather.

Parking.

The microphone that worked yesterday and is now possessed.

Start small.

A successful room of thirty people is better than an empty room built for two hundred.

Live events should grow from real audience connection, not your fantasy of what a successful show is supposed to do.

## The Trust Filter

Before any money decision, ask:

Does this fit the audience?

Would I be comfortable explaining this relationship?

Is the disclosure clear?

Does the sponsor make sense?

Is the ad load reasonable?

Does this make the show sustainable without making it worse?

Would I still respect the show if I were listening?

If the answer is no, slow down.

A quick check can save a long regret.

## Closing Thought

Money matters. Trust matters more. If you build a show people care about, money has somewhere to stand. If you chase money before trust, the whole thing wobbles.

# Chapter 22: Make the Show Bigger Than the Episode

## Newsletters, clips, communities, events, books, workshops, archives, and the world around the show.

A lot of creators think the episode is the whole thing.

Record episode.

Edit episode.

Upload episode.

Post episode.

Repeat until either success arrives or your soul leaves your body.

That is one way to do it.

But a strong show can become bigger than the episode.

Not immediately.

Not before the show knows what it is.

Not because some content marketer with perfect teeth said every creator needs a funnel.

But because a good show creates more than recordings.

It creates ideas.

Moments.

Stories.

Questions.

Relationships.

Audience habits.

Guest relationships.

Sponsor value.

Community memory.

A body of work.

A world.

That world can become a newsletter, live event, book, course, community, archive, workshop, social series, video channel, documentary, stage show, product, service, or something you do not even see yet.

The episode is the anchor.

But it does not have to be the entire boat.

And yes, that metaphor is probably a little nautical for a podcast book, but we are keeping it.

## The Episode Is the Campfire

Think of the episode as the campfire.

People gather around it.

They listen.

They watch.

They laugh.

They learn.

They remember.

They argue.

They feel something.

But the campfire can create other things.

Stories told around it.

People who meet because of it.

Food cooked over it.

A reason to come back.

A place people remember.

That is what a show can become.

If all you do is light the campfire and then immediately run away to light the next one, you may miss what is happening around it.

Pay attention.

What questions do people ask after the episode?

What stories do they send?

What clips do they share?

What guests do they suggest?

What sponsors fit naturally?

What topics keep coming back?

What audience need is bigger than the episode?

That is where the bigger show begins.

## Clips Are Doors

We have talked about clips before, but here they matter again.

A clip is a door.

It is not the house.

A good clip gives someone a reason to step inside the show.

That means the clip should make sense on its own but point back to something bigger.

A funny moment.

A strong line.

A useful tip.

A surprising story.

A guest confession.

A local memory.

A before-and-after.

A sharp opinion.

That clip can live on YouTube Shorts, Instagram, Facebook, TikTok, LinkedIn, X, your website, your newsletter, or wherever your audience actually is.

But do not make clips like you are feeding pigeons.

Randomly throwing little pieces everywhere and hoping something happens.

Be intentional.

What is the door?

Where does it lead?

If a person likes this clip, what should they do next?

Watch the full episode?

Join the email list?

Send a story?

Download a worksheet?

Buy a ticket?

Check out the sponsor?

The clip should have a path.

Otherwise, you are just giving the feed another snack.

## The Newsletter Is the Living Room

If the episode is the campfire and the clips are doors, the newsletter is the living room.

It is more direct.

More personal.

Less algorithmic.

A place where people who care can hear from you without waiting for a platform to decide whether you are worthy today.

A newsletter does not have to be complicated.

It can be simple.

"Here is this week's episode."

"Here is why we made it."

"Here is the best moment."

"Here is a question for you."

"Here is what is coming next."

That is enough.

The newsletter can also become a companion.

Behind-the-scenes notes.

Guest links.

Extra resources.

Listener stories.

Questions for upcoming episodes.

Sponsor offers.

Event announcements.

First looks.

Bonus thoughts.

The key is that the newsletter should feel like part of the show, not just a flyer for the show.

A flyer says, "New episode out."

A companion says, "Here is what I have been thinking about since we recorded."

That is different.

The second one builds relationship.

## The Website Is the Archive

Your website is where the show becomes findable and organized.

A feed is chronological.

A website can be useful.

That is the difference.

A podcast feed says, “Here is the newest thing.”

A website can say:

Start here.

Best episodes for beginners.

Episodes about AI.

Episodes about storytelling.

Sponsor information.

Guest information.

Local history archive.

Family story archive.

Resources.

Worksheets.

Transcripts.

Topic hubs.

Recommended tools.

Events.

Contact.

The website is where the show stops being a pile and becomes a library.

That matters more over time.

The bigger the show gets, the more important organization becomes.

If you have fifty episodes and no structure, new people do not know where to begin.

If you have topic hubs, starter guides, transcripts, and clear pages, the show becomes easier to enter.

And if AI search keeps changing how people discover things, a clear website gives the internet something to understand.

Do not hide your show from the future.

Give it an archive.

## Listener Questions Are Content

Listener questions are gold.

They tell you what people care about.

They reveal confusion.

They create episodes.

They make the audience feel included.

They also help you avoid making the show only from your own head.

A listener question can become:

A segment.

A short episode.

A newsletter answer.

A clip.

A blog post.

A worksheet.

A guest prompt.

A live event topic.

A product idea.

A workshop.

If one person asks it, others may be wondering it.

Create a clear way for people to send questions.

Email.

Form.

Voicemail.

Text line.

Social comments.

Community group.

Whatever fits.

Then use the questions.

Give credit when appropriate.

Protect privacy when needed.

And say thank you.

A show becomes stronger when the audience knows they can shape it.

Not control it.

Shape it.

There is a difference.

## Community Stories Are Fuel

If your show is local, legacy, mission-driven, nostalgic, educational, or built around lived experience, community stories can become fuel.

Ask people:

What do you remember?

What did that place mean to you?

What did you learn the hard way?

What was your first job?

What show shaped you?

What local business do you miss?

What technology made you feel old for the first time?

What story from your family should not disappear?

What did you try that actually worked?

These responses can become episodes.

Or segments.

Or social posts.

Or website archives.

Or live readings.

Or a book.

Or a documentary.

Or a newsletter series.

This is where the show becomes more than a broadcast.

It becomes a collection point.

People like being asked.

They like remembering.

They like contributing to something that feels real.

Do not waste that.

## Guests Are Not One-Time Transactions

A guest should not always disappear after the episode.

Some guests become partners.

Some become recurring voices.

Some become live event panelists.

Some introduce sponsors.

Some bring other guests.

Some share the show for months.

Some become part of the larger world.

Treat guests well.

Send them the episode.

Send clips.

Thank them.

Tag them.

Give them clean links.

Follow up later.

Tell them how the episode performed if it makes sense.

Invite them back when there is a reason.

A guest relationship can be more valuable than a single download spike.

Especially for business, local, niche, and community shows.

The episode is one touchpoint.

The relationship is bigger.

## Sponsors Can Be Part of the World, Not Just Ads

A good sponsor does not have to feel bolted on.

The right sponsor can become part of the show world.

A local coffee shop sponsoring a local history show.

A community bank sponsoring stories about small businesses.

A software company sponsoring an AI-for-creators show.

A theater sponsoring an audio fiction series.

A bookstore sponsoring author interviews.

A venue sponsoring live recordings.

A sponsor can support the world around the show.

Not just interrupt the episode.

That might include:

Episode reads.

Website placement.

Newsletter mentions.

Live event presence.

Resource guides.

Sponsored segments.

Community projects.

Contest support.

Audience discounts.

Scholarships or giveaways.

But be careful.

The sponsor should fit.

If the sponsor feels wrong, the audience will feel it.

Sponsorship is not only money.

It is association.

Choose associations carefully.

## Live Events Make the Show Physical

Live events can change the relationship with the audience.

A show is usually in someone's ears or on a screen.

A live event makes it physical.

People show up.

They see each other.

They meet the host.

They talk.

They laugh in the same room.

They buy a drink.

They ask a question.

They realize the audience is real.

That can be powerful.

A live event does not have to be huge.

In fact, start small.

A live recording with thirty people.

A panel.

A workshop.

A listening party.

A storytelling night.

A local history night.

A sponsor-backed meetup.

A launch party.

A season finale.

A class.

A community conversation.

A small good room is better than a large sad room.

Trust me.

Nothing humbles a person faster than too many empty chairs.

Start with the room you can fill.

Then grow.

## Workshops and Classes

If your show teaches anything, workshops may be a natural extension.

A show about podcasting can become a workshop on starting your first show.

A show about AI can become a class for small business owners.

A local history show can become a preservation workshop.

A business show can become a client training.

A storytelling show can become a memoir or family-history class.

A media literacy show can become a school or community program.

The show builds trust.

The workshop gives people a deeper experience.

This can also be a revenue path that does not depend on massive downloads.

You do not need a million listeners to fill a room with twenty people who need help.

That is important.

Smaller, deeper offers can work better than chasing giant reach.

## A Show Can Become a Book

We should probably mention this because, well, here we are.

A show can become a book.

Not automatically.

Not by dumping transcripts into a document and calling it a manuscript like nobody will notice.

But a show can create the raw material.

Ideas.

Stories.

Frameworks.

Listener questions.

Guest lessons.

Examples.

Language.

Chapters.

A show teaches you what you keep saying.

A book organizes it.

If you record enough episodes around a clear promise, you may start seeing the book inside the show.

The same can work the other way.

A book can become a show.

Each chapter can become an episode.

Each worksheet can become a segment.

Each reader question can become content.

Each concept can become a clip.

The book and show can feed each other.

That is not cheating.

That is building a world.

## A Show Can Become a Course or Resource Library

If the show solves problems, it can become a resource library.

Not every listener wants a course.

But some may want a structured path.

A show is often nonlinear.

A course or guide can say:

Do this first.

Then this.

Then this.

Use this worksheet.

Watch this lesson.

Download this template.

Ask this question.

For a teaching show, a course may be a natural next step.

For a business show, a resource library may support clients.

For a community show, an archive may preserve information.

For a creator show, a toolkit may help people act.

Again, the show creates trust.

The resource gives structure.

Do not build the course too early.

Make sure people actually want it.

Audience questions will tell you.

If people keep asking the same thing, that may be a resource.

If people keep getting stuck in the same place, that may be a worksheet.

If one episode keeps getting shared, that may be a workshop.

Pay attention.

## Merch Is Not Mandatory

Let's talk about merch.

Everybody gets excited about merch.

T-shirts.

Mugs.

Stickers.

Hats.

Posters.

All fun.

Also, not always necessary.

Merch works when the show has identity strong enough that people want to wear it or put it on something.

That requires more than a logo.

It requires belonging.

A phrase.

A joke.

A symbol.

A local connection.

A fandom.

A mission.

A memory.

Do not launch merch just because other shows have merch.

You may end up with a box of shirts in your garage, sitting next to old Christmas decorations and that appliance you swear you are going to fix.

Merch should come when the audience wants to represent the show.

Not when the creator wants proof the show is real.

## Social Platforms Are Outposts

Social platforms are outposts.

Not the whole kingdom.

Use them.

Do not live and die by them.

Each platform can serve a role.

YouTube: full episodes, clips, search, video discovery.

Facebook: local/community sharing, older audiences, groups.

Instagram: clips, visuals, behind the scenes, guest graphics.

LinkedIn: business authority, practical clips, professional guests.

TikTok: discovery, short-form personality, fast hooks.

X: real-time commentary, niche conversations, media people yelling into the weather.

Use the platforms that fit the show.

Do not chase every platform because you are afraid of missing out.

Missing out is not the worst thing.

Burning out because you tried to feed six platforms with no team might be worse.

Pick your outposts.

Maintain them.

Send people back to the show world.

## The Show World Map

Eventually, draw a map of the show world.

At the center: the show.

Around it:

Website.

Email list.

Clips.

Social platforms.

Guest network.

Sponsors.

Live events.

Worksheets.

Resource library.

Community stories.

Products.

Services.

Book.

Workshops.

Archive.

Not all at once.

Do not look at this and think you need everything by Friday.

This is not a to-do list.

It is a possibility map.

The point is to see how one show can create many paths.

Some paths will make sense.

Some will not.

Some may come years later.

Some may never come.

But if you understand the world around the show, you stop treating each episode like an isolated chore.

You start building.

## Do Not Build the World Before the Show

This is the warning.

Do not build a giant show world before the show works.

Do not create a community before you have people.

Do not create merch before you have identity.

Do not create a course before you know the problem.

Do not create a live event before you know who would come.

Do not build a massive website before you have a clear promise.

Do not create seventeen content channels before you can publish one episode consistently.

Build in order.

Show first.

Audience second.

World third.

Or maybe:

Promise first.

Episode second.

Relationship third.

Expansion fourth.

The show world should grow from real signals.

Not fantasy.

Fantasy is fun, but it will absolutely let you order 200 mugs nobody asked for.

## The Flywheel

A good show ecosystem creates a flywheel.

The episode creates clips.

Clips bring people to the show.

The show brings people to the email list.

The email list brings questions.

Questions create episodes.

Episodes attract guests.

Guests bring audiences.

Audience response attracts sponsors.

Sponsors support better production.

Better production creates stronger episodes.

Stronger episodes create better clips.

That is a flywheel.

Not everything works perfectly.

This is not a motivational diagram in a hotel conference room.

But the idea is useful.

A show can create motion when the parts connect.

If the parts do not connect, you just have tasks.

Episode.

Clip.

Post.

Email.

Website.

Sponsor.

All separate.

Exhausting.

Connect them.

Make each piece help the next piece.

That is how the show becomes bigger without simply becoming more work.

## The Danger of Expansion

Expansion can be exciting.

It can also kill the show.

Every new thing needs care.

Newsletter.

Event.

Community.

Workshop.

Course.

Merch.

Book.

Sponsor program.

YouTube channel.

Each one takes time.

Each one creates expectations.

Each one can pull energy from the core show.

So before adding anything, ask:

Does this serve the audience?

Does this serve the show promise?

Does this create energy or only consume it?

Can we maintain it?

Is there a clear next action for the audience?

Does this support the business or mission?

What can we stop doing if we add this?

That last question matters.

If you add and never subtract, you eventually collapse under your own good ideas.

A lot of creators do not run out of ideas.

They run out of capacity.

Be careful.

## Closing Thought

The episode matters.

Do not misunderstand me.

Make good episodes.

Respect the episode.

Structure it.

Edit it.

Title it clearly.

Publish it well.

But do not stop seeing what the episode can create.

A strong show can become more than a feed.

It can become a world.

A place where people ask questions.

A place where stories gather.

A place where sponsors fit.

A place where events happen.

A place where a newsletter feels personal.

A place where clips are doors.

A place where a website becomes an archive.

A place where a book, course, workshop, or community can grow naturally.

Do not force it.

Do not overbuild it.

Do not order the mugs too early.

But pay attention.

The show may be bigger than the episode.

Let it become bigger in the right order.

Start with the promise.

Make the show.

Earn the audience.

Then build the world around it.

# Chapter 23: Let AI Carry Some of the Weight

AI is here. We can argue about it, complain about it, be amazed by it, be annoyed by it, or pretend it is not changing things. But it is here.

If you are making a show now, you need to understand what AI can do, what it should not do, and where it can actually help.

AI is a tool. Powerful, strange, sometimes brilliant, sometimes confidently wrong while wearing a nice blazer. But still a tool.

The show is the show. The story is the story. The voice is the voice.

## AI Should Reduce Friction

AI should make the show easier to make, clearer, or more sustainable. If it makes you sound generic, fake, or like every other person using the same lazy prompt, it is not helping.

The goal is not to replace your voice. The goal is to get your voice out into the world with less drag.

## Before Recording

AI can help with the blank page. Ask it for episode ideas, outlines, guest questions, audience objections, examples, or ways to organize messy notes.

It gives you something to react to. Sometimes the answer is good. Sometimes it is bad enough that you suddenly know what you really wanted. That counts.

Use AI as a pre-production assistant, not the boss. It can help you ask: what is the episode promise, who is it for, what does the listener need, what are the three main points, what stories should be included, and what might become a clip?

Do not read the AI outline word for word unless you enjoy sounding like a webinar that became self-aware.

## Research With Supervision

AI can summarize, suggest angles, explain complicated topics, compare sources, and build background notes. It can also be wrong. Very wrong. Wrong with confidence.

Verify names, dates, quotes, statistics, legal claims, medical claims, financial claims, and anything that could embarrass you or mislead the audience.

AI is a research assistant that needs supervision.

## After Recording

After recording, AI can help with the tired part: titles, summaries, show notes, transcripts, chapter markers, clips, social posts, newsletter copy, YouTube descriptions, guest share copy, and sponsor recaps.

Give it the transcript. Ask for key takeaways, possible clips, useful quotes, and episode descriptions. Then rewrite in your voice.

AI may miss the best moment. It may smooth out the human part. It may write social posts that sound like a LinkedIn robot got promoted. Use it. Then fix it.

## Clips and Consistency

AI can help find strong moments, but it cannot create moments that do not exist. If the episode is mush, the clipping tool will just find smaller mush.

AI can also help consistency: weekly checklists, show notes templates, guest emails, publishing reminders, social templates, sponsor copy, and clip captions.

If podfade is often a system problem, AI can help strengthen the system.

## The Human Layer

Before publishing AI-assisted material, ask: Does this sound like me? Is it true? Is it useful? Is it specific? Is there a real example? Would I say this out loud?

AI is great at average. You are not trying to be average.

## Ethics

Do not use AI to fake people, clone voices without permission, create fake endorsements, make guests say things they did not say, hide paid relationships, publish unverified claims, or use private information carelessly.

A show is built on trust. AI should not be the thing that wrecks it.

## The Prompt Formula

If you want better AI output, give better instructions.

A weak prompt:

"Write show notes."

A better prompt:

"You are helping produce a practical, conversational show for first-time creators over forty-five. Read this transcript and write show notes in a warm, plainspoken tone. Avoid hype. Include a short summary, five key takeaways, links mentioned, one listener question, and one clear call to action."

Better input gets better output.

Use this formula:

Role.

Audience.

Task.

Tone.

Format.

Constraints.

Example:

"You are a producer helping with a Gen X-focused creator show. The audience is people who remember the old media world and want to use new tools without feeling stupid. Create ten interview questions for a guest who started a business after fifty. Keep questions story-based, practical, and not too corporate."

That gives AI a job.

It is not mind-reading.

Tell it what good looks like.

## The Prompt Library

Do not start from scratch every week.

Create reusable prompts for:

Episode brainstorming.

Episode outlines.

Guest research.

Interview questions.

Transcript summaries.

Clip finding.

Show notes.

Episode titles.

Newsletter blurbs.

Social posts.

Sponsor reads.

SEO descriptions.

Audience feedback analysis.

Save the prompts that work.

Improve them.

Name them.

Keep them in the show bible.

This becomes part of your system.

The more repeatable your AI workflow is, the less likely you are to misuse it out of panic.

## Fact-Checking Routine

When AI helps with research, create a fact-checking routine.

Highlight every name, date, statistic, quote, legal claim, medical claim, financial claim, historical claim, and anything that could make you look foolish if wrong.

Then verify.

Use primary sources where possible.

Official pages.

Original documents.

Reputable reporting.

Actual interviews.

Your own notes.

Do not let AI's confidence become your confidence.

AI can sound like it knows.

That is not the same as knowing.

A show earns trust when it treats facts carefully.

## Keeping Your Voice

After AI drafts anything, add the human layer.

Ask:

Where is my actual opinion?

Where is my example?

Where is the line only I would say?

Where does this sound too smooth?

Where does this sound like a brochure?

Where does this need a story?

Where does this need less polish and more truth?

Then rewrite.

AI is often good at making things neat.

But neat is not always memorable.

The audience does not come for neat.

They come for useful, specific, human, and true.

## Privacy and Guests

Be careful what you feed into AI tools.

Guest emails.

Private stories.

Unreleased episodes.

Sensitive business information.

Legal matters.

Health information.

Personal family details.

Anything confidential.

Think before uploading.

Use tools and settings that fit the level of privacy you need.

When in doubt, remove personal details or get permission.

The show is built on trust.

That includes behind-the-scenes trust.

## Closing Thought

AI can help carry the bricks. It cannot decide why you are building the house.

Use the tool to carry weight. You still carry the meaning.

# Chapter 24: Build the Show You Can Keep Making

Starting is hard. Keeping going is harder.

A show is not built on launch energy. A show is built on repeatability. Can you do it again? Can you do it next week? Can you do it when work gets busy, the guest cancels, the numbers are flat, and the dog chooses violence during recording?

Do not just build the show you can start. Build the show you can keep making.

## Your Actual Life

Your show has to survive your real life. Not your fantasy life where your calendar is open, your computer behaves, everyone in the house respects your recording time, and all the remotes have batteries.

Build for the life you actually have. A lot of people design a show for the person they wish they were. Do not do that.

## Consistency Does Not Always Mean Weekly

Weekly can be great. But consistency means the audience knows what to expect and you can deliver it. That might be weekly, every other week, monthly, seasonal, a limited series, or a monthly live show with clips between.

Make a promise you can keep.

## Seasons Are Not Cheating

Some shows should be seasonal. Seasons let you plan, batch, take breaks, and make the rhythm clear. A planned break feels professional. An unplanned disappearance feels like the host fell into a well.

Television understood seasons. We forgot, somehow, and decided every creator must publish forever until the algorithm personally sends flowers.

## Batching and Buffers

Batching saves shows. Record two solo episodes in one afternoon. Schedule three interviews in a day. Record a full short season before launch. Batch intros, outros, clips, or social posts.

A buffer protects you from life. If you are always recording the day before release, you are one flat tire away from missing.

## Make It Smaller Before You Quit

When a show gets heavy, most people think they have two options: keep doing the full version or quit. There is a third option: make it smaller.

Shorter episodes. Fewer segments. Less editing. No video for a while. Fewer platforms. A simpler intro. A replay with new commentary. Every-other-week publishing. One clip instead of five.

Do not burn down the house because one room is too hot.

## Protect the Part You Love

Every show has a part that gives energy and a part that drains energy. Maybe you love conversation but hate editing. Maybe you love research but hate social posting. Maybe you love live shows but hate weekly production.

Protect the part you love. Simplify the part that drains you. That is not weakness. That is design.

## Checklists, Templates, and Rest

A checklist saves your show from your mood. Templates stop you from reinventing the same wheel while the wagon is on fire.

Rest is not quitting. Rest is maintenance. Build rest into the system before your body forces it into the system.

## The Ten-Episode Review

After ten episodes, review calmly. What worked? What dragged? What gave you energy? What wore you out? Is the format right? Is video helping? What should stop? What should grow?

The first ten episodes are not just content. They are research. The best kind — the kind that comes from doing.

## Three Sustainable Models

Here are three models that can work.

**The Weekly Light Model**

Shorter episodes, simple format, limited editing, one or two promotion actions. Good for commentary, education, local updates, and personality shows.

**The Biweekly Quality Model**

More prep, stronger editing, better guest process, more polished pages and clips. Good for interviews and practical teaching shows.

**The Seasonal Model**

Record and produce a batch around one theme. Launch as a season. Take a planned break. Good for audio fiction, documentary, true crime, history, or deep-dive teaching.

None of these is morally superior.

The right model is the one the show can survive.

## Standard Operating Procedures

A standard operating procedure sounds corporate.

I know.

Stay with me.

It is just a written way of doing the thing.

How to record.

How to name files.

How to edit.

How to publish.

How to write show notes.

How to send guest prep.

How to make clips.

How to send sponsor recaps.

This matters even if you are alone.

Because one day you may get help.

And even before that, you are helping future you.

Future you will not remember every step.

Future you will be tired.

Give future you instructions.

## Delegation and Help

You do not have to do everything forever.

Maybe you start alone.

Fine.

But if the show grows, look for help.

Editing.

Show notes.

Clip creation.

Guest booking.

Artwork.

Website updates.

Sponsor outreach.

Social posting.

AI workflow setup.

Even a little help can change the whole energy of the show.

If money is tight, trade may help.

If you have a network, share tasks.

If you have a co-host, divide the work clearly.

Do not silently carry everything and then resent everyone.

That is not leadership.

That is how group projects went bad in high school.

Communicate.

Assign.

Simplify.

## Protecting Relationships

Your show should not make everyone around you hate your show.

If recording time affects family, talk about it.

If you need quiet, explain it.

If you are always editing during dinner, that is a problem.

If your spouse only hears about the show when you are stressed, that is a problem.

If the people around you feel like the show is taking you away from them, pay attention.

Creative work matters.

So do people.

Build boundaries.

Build support.

Build rest.

Do not make the show the villain in your house.

A show that ruins your life is not a good show.

It is a problem with an RSS feed.

## The Review Meeting

Every ten episodes, have a review meeting.

Even if it is just you.

Ask:

What worked?

What drained me?

What audience response mattered?

What should I stop doing?

What should become easier?

What should become better?

What should I keep exactly the same?

What did I learn about the audience?

What did I learn about myself?

Then make decisions.

Not panic changes.

Not mood changes.

Decisions.

The review meeting is where the show grows up.

## Closing Thought

A show that ruins your life is not a good show. It is a problem with an RSS feed.

Make it smaller, seasonal, batched, templated, rested, and real enough to last.

# Chapter 25: Start Simple. Tell the Truth. Keep Going.

Here is what I hope you understand by now.

You do not need to be famous to make a show. You do not need to be young. You do not need to be a tech genius. You do not need a perfect studio. You do not need a giant audience on day one.

You need something worth saying. You need a clear enough idea. You need a listener or viewer in mind. You need a simple system. You need enough courage to start before you feel completely ready. Then you need to keep going long enough to get better.

Not easy. But simple.

## The Tools Are Not the Point

The tools are amazing. You can record from home, interview someone across the country, edit on a laptop, publish to the world, make artwork, create clips, use AI, build a website, send an email list, sell a sponsorship, and reach people you never would have reached before.

That is incredible.

But the tools are not the point. A microphone does not make a show. A camera does not make a show. A hosting platform does not make a show. AI does not make a show.

You do.

Your taste, judgment, curiosity, humor, experience, questions, and willingness to make the thing.

Do not confuse access with meaning. We have more access than ever. Now we have to make something that matters.

## Somebody Needs What You Know

Somebody needs the story you almost did not tell because you thought it was too ordinary. Somebody needs the lesson you learned the hard way. Somebody needs the explanation that only makes sense because you lived through it.

We live in a world full of content, but not always full of connection. There is plenty of noise, polish, generic advice, and AI-written mush with no fingerprints on it.

What there is not enough of is honest voice. Specific experience. Real stories. People telling the truth in a way another person can recognize.

That is your advantage. Not that you know every trick. Your advantage is that you have lived.

Use that.

## Start Small Without Thinking Small

Starting small does not mean thinking small. A small first episode can still be part of a big vision. A simple audio setup can still become a serious show. A ten-person audience can still become a loyal audience. A house ad can still train the show to feel sponsor-ready.

The first version is not there to impress the world. The first version is there to teach you.

Then you make the second version better. And the third. And the tenth.

## Do Not Wait for Permission

Nobody is coming to give you permission. Nobody is going to review your life experience and decide you are now officially allowed to make a show.

You decide. You decide the story matters enough to try. You decide the first version is allowed to be rough. You decide the starter setup is good enough. You decide to publish before you can talk yourself out of it again.

You are allowed to begin. Right now. With what you have. Where you are. As who you are.

## The Show Is a Promise

A show says: give me your time, and I will give you something back.

Knowledge. Laughter. A story. Comfort. A warning. Perspective. A place to belong. A reminder that someone else sees the world the way you do.

If you keep that promise enough times, trust begins to form. That is the real value. Not just downloads, views, sponsors, or clips.

Trust.

## The First Episode Is Waiting

Eventually, planning has to become an episode. Not another article. Not another gear review. Not another debate about the name. Not another pass through the artwork. Not another AI prompt.

At some point, you sit down and make the show.

Record the test. Write the outline. Call the guest. Press the button. Talk. Listen back. Fix what you can. Publish when it is ready enough. Then make the next one.

Simple. Terrifying. Worth it.

## The 72-Hour Start

Here is a simple challenge.

Within the next seventy-two hours, do one thing that makes the show more real.

The companion workbook — worksheets, checklists, and templates for everything in this book — is at **thatmikehamilton.com/workbook**. Print it, fill it in, lose it, print it again. That is what it is for.

Not ten things.

One.

Write the one-sentence show promise.

Record a five-minute test.

List ten episodes.

Email one possible guest.

Pick three possible names.

Create a rough cover concept.

Make the folder structure.

Draft the intro.

Fill out the Final Launch Card.

Do one thing.

Then do the next.

Do not let the end of this book become another place where the idea rests.

Books can become hiding places too.

You read the book.

You feel inspired.

You tell yourself you are “getting ready.”

Then two months later the book is under a stack of mail and nothing has happened.

Do not do that.

Use the book.

Mark it up.

Steal the templates.

Argue with the advice.

Make your own version.

But do something.

## A Letter to Future You

In the workbook (thatmikehamilton.com/workbook), there is a page for a note to future you.

The you who will get tired.

The you who will miss a week.

The you who will hate an episode.

The you who will compare numbers.

The you who will wonder if any of this matters.

Tell that person why you started.

Tell that person what the show is for.

Tell that person what can be simplified before quitting.

Tell that person that a bad week is not a dead show.

That letter may sound cheesy.

Write it anyway.

Sometimes future you needs to hear from the person who still believed.

## The Legacy Part

Not every show becomes a business.

Not every show gets sponsors.

Not every show gets a big audience.

But some shows still matter deeply.

A show can document family stories.

A show can capture a community.

A show can teach what you know.

A show can preserve a voice.

A show can become a record of a season of life.

A show can help one person.

A show can make you feel creative again.

Do not reduce the value of the show only to money or numbers.

Those things can matter.

But they are not the only things.

Sometimes the value is that the thing exists.

A voice recorded.

A story told.

A lesson passed on.

A person heard.

That matters too.

## The Last Push

You are allowed to be new.

You are allowed to start small.

You are allowed to use simple gear.

You are allowed to hate your voice at first.

You are allowed to change the show after ten episodes.

You are allowed to use AI for help.

You are allowed to ask for sponsors when the show has value.

You are allowed to rest.

You are allowed to come back.

You are allowed to make the thing before you fully understand the whole industry.

That is how most things get made.

Not by knowing everything.

By starting.

Then learning.

Then adjusting.

Then continuing.

Open the notebook.

Press record.

Send the email.

Make the show.

## Closing Thought

Make the show.

Not because it will be perfect. Not because it will be easy. Not because it will make you famous.

Make it because something in you keeps asking to be made. Make it because you have carried the story long enough. Make it because the tools are here, the gatekeepers are fewer, and the cost of trying is lower than it has ever been.

Make it because you are not done.

Start simple.

Tell the truth.

Keep going.

www.ingramcontent.com/pod-product-compliance
Lightning Source LLC
LaVergne TN
LVHW100723061126
851857LV00011B/375
*9798905996269*